4 —

THE CHILDREN OF DARKNESS

THE CHILDREN OF DARKNESS

by Richard S. Wheeler

Arlington House   New Rochelle, N. Y.

Manufactured in the United States of America

Library of Congress Cataloging in Publication Data

Wheeler, Richard S.
    Children of darkness.

    1. Youth—Conduct of life. 2. Youth—
United States. 3. United States—Religion.
4. Secularism—United States. I. Title.
BJ1661.W44   170'.202'23   73-8800
ISBN 0-87000-208-2

CONTENTS

THE CHILDREN OF DARKNESS

1. THESIS

CHEEK by jowl in our western societies are people with totally diverse outlooks on life: in the breast of one man is a profound belief in life hereafter; in the heart of another is the certitude that one must live his threescore years and ten to the hilt, because there will be no more life. Some believe in God; some don't. Some adhere to the Ten Commandments; many don't. Some try to practice the Golden Rule; others are out to get whatever they can. Some believe in chastity; many do not. Some believe that Christian morals and ethics are the cement that binds people together in society. Others believe such bridles on behavior cause deep neuroses, hang-ups, and inhibitions that prevent the natural man from enjoying life.

In short, the schism between believers and nonbelievers runs deep and is growing deeper. Side by side, in jobs, on the streets, in neighborhoods, in families, are people who have little to share with their intimates: agnostic sons of devout parents; swinging daughters of chaste mothers; acid-head children of teetotalers, and, occasionally, virtuous progeny of debauched parents. We take all this for granted but we shouldn't. We suppose such diversity is the natural fruit of a free and heterogeneous society, but it isn't natural. In fact, it is wildly improbable and one of the miracles of the times is that the United States remains reasonably stable amidst the schisms and chasms growing so wide and deep that people can no longer reach across them.

There are innumerable faults running through the bedrock of the Republic: the partisan conflicts of Republicans and Democrats; the deep antagonisms between liberals and conservatives; the abrading generations (about which this book will have much to say); the old bitternesses between black and white, North and South, and the ethnic groups in the cities. Of these, perhaps the most embracing is the liberal-conservative struggle, because each warring ideology contains a broad, deep concept of the ordering of society. But infinitely deeper than all these is the struggle between secular people and the religious. Most, if not all, of the lesser conflicts are merely facets of the central struggle between the faithful and the skeptical. It is religion that has informed and guided the West for two millennia, and the Jews for five millennia, a religion that involves a faith and commitment that transcend the merely human allegiances arrayed against it.

It is generally true that liberalism and the progessivist left are, derivatively, the political expressions of secularism, while conservatism and the right are political expressions of the older religious values. But I hasten to add caveats: there are deeply religious political liberals; there are agnostic conservatives. There are liberal Protestants who accept a modernistic demythologized religion as well as the traditional social values of the West. There are conservatives who are pure secularists seeking to dump all remaining moral restraints in the name of libertarian freedoms. And yet . . . and yet . . . all things considered, the thesis stands. Empirically, one simply discovers that the bulk of secular men and skeptics cluster around the banners of the left, and the bulk of devout men rally under the flags of the right. If conservatism is not expressly the politics of religion, it is, at least, the expression of the *values*, *ethics,* and *morals* derived from religious beliefs.

The conflict between faith and skepticism is unbridgeable and irreconcilable. One cannot simultaneously accept God and the divinity of Jesus Christ and yet believe that God is unprovable or nonexistent. Nor can one behave in harmony with each viewpoint simultaneously. A religious man orders his existence and places checks on his passions in a way that evolves a character fundamentally different from the secular man, who places fewer checks on himself, and pursues different life-goals. There are straddlers, of course. But they are in trouble through all their days, vacillating between one code and the other, piling guilt and anxiety and conflict upon their heads. Christians do things that are irrational to secular men: secular men do things that the Christian regards as sin, or as a poor substitute for his own values. The wretched ones in the middle, unable to accept or reject faith, are the true sufferers.

Across the spectrum, ranging from faith at one end to skepticism at the other are broad areas of inner spiritual experience that separate men and brothers from one another, and provide radically differing outlooks. At the secular end is what is theologically known as natural man. At the religious end is the spiritual man who has managed to tame his carnal impulses and impose a spiritual character on the natural one. And in the middle is the suffering multitude who are at war with themselves, accepting the natural man, but not enough to resolve these conflicting hungers and achieve an inner peace.

The secular thrust is toward the creation of natural man, i.e., men who do not have a strongly internalized sense of guilt and whose interest is to do pretty much as they please. Natural men are whole men. They are not usually at war with themselves. They achieve their inner unity by denying the legitimacy of most social restraint as well as internalized restraint in the form of conscience. They regard the state, religion, custom, and tradition as essentially oppressive because they are inhibiting and induce guilt. Their goal is a life devoid of guilt or shame. Numerous psychiatrists agree with this ultimate personal goal and direct their therapy toward alleviating the hang-ups of their patients. The natural man achieves wholeness only by setting himself permanently at odds with the demands of society. He becomes, in other words, a liberal, or a man of the left, forever warring against restraints, against the things that seem to bind him down. Even so, he generally agrees that some restraints against violence and theft are necessary for the smooth progress of society, but even these are clear threats to his individuality, his right to do his thing untrammeled by the world's fogeys. Much of the youth movement is grounded in the vision of the natural man; the man who plays and works without guilt; the man who is the enemy of the repressive past.

However, the natural man may well be an antisocial man. He has no strong internal governing mechanism to regulate his conduct and is wont to rip off what he needs, and hurt others casually. He is governable only by sheer force, i.e., by a state regime that will check him with the threat of violence, or incarceration. It is true that liberalism contains a code of defined rights and boundaries, but it is noteworthy that this code is not something internalized by natural men, but external, embodied in law.

In the middle range, somewhere between natural and spiritual man, lies the bulk of Americans, and especially the bourgeoisie. This broad group is generally among the most stable and fruitful, although filled with inward conflict and restlessness. It is stable because it possesses inner discipline and recognizes legitimate authority. It is dynamic because its members are continually at war with themselves, balancing off the claims of conscience against the weight of natural impulse. In the middle range are persons who feel guilty and anxious, and unable to relieve their guilt or resolve their anxiety. Some are devout and fill the pews every Sunday. But their faith is ritual and incomplete, and their religion tends to be a once-a-week thing. It is this middle group, that can't reconcile natural temptations with conscience, that is the hotbed of neuroses and worse disorders.

Increasingly, as the gulf deepens between secular and religious men, those in the middle will have to leap to one side or the other. Most are drifting toward the pure secular life, but a few are consciously vaulting back to the world of faith. For instance, as secular men push farther toward uninhibited expression, which they believe is natural and good, they produce works that the faithful must regard as pornographic or obscene. In the end, as such material becomes increasingly frank, a man must take sides, either for restraints or for free expression. The secular and religious men each know where they stand; those in the middle can only carom from titillation to disapproval. There are other issues, such as abortion and divorce, church taxation, and classroom prayer, that must force these semi-Christians or casual secularists in some direction. Eventually the gulf between the Kingdom and Heaven and the Kingdom of the World will be too wide for their high-wire act.

At the religious end of the spectrum is spiritual man, whose union with God is profound and joyous. His carnal self has been not merely suppressed but virtually obliterated. He, like natural man, is whole and freed from guilt. He is not at war with himself because he has accepted God's forgiveness and subordinated all else to his faith. He is a saint. He has internalized government. In society he is, perforce, a self-governing citizen who needs neither restraint nor prodding to be honest, truthful, and charitable among his fellows. In a just society and under a just government he is a model citizen whose word is bond and whose concern for others is constantly manifest.

However, the spiritual man's victory over his passions is always provisional and depends on a daily renewal of his union with God. It is commonplace for the best of spiritual men to falter—to become natural men for a duration—during moments of stress. The spiritual man is, precisely, unnatural, and the spiritual nature is sometimes a weak master over natural instinct. The result is not a bitter or shriveled personality, as some would suppose, but joy, self-discipline, and an ability to swallow up weaknesses. The most notable quality of spiritual men is their radiance and joy, their constant celebration of victory over death. It is the goal of every Christian to be born into the spiritual life, though few achieve that elevated status. The character of spiritual men varies profoundly from that of natural men: the spiritual man enjoys serving his fellows while the natural man is doomed to pursue mainly selfish goals. Spiritual man can say no to himself, while natural man can say no only to others and society.

The evolution of such deeply different types of personality among American peoples has been a long time developing. Indeed, the conflict between secular and religious believers antedates the New World. There is a temptation to date the origins of the secular, skeptical spirit to the dawning of the Renaissance. But in fact the deepest flowering of Christian faith was still in the future, spurred by the fierce competition of nascent Protestantism and the Mother Church. The much maligned Puritans, for example, were yet to come, carrying within them a totally theological existence. Such persons lived their spiritual life with an intensity not witnessed since the primitive church. In some respects the Reformation and the centuries immediately thereafter witnessed a broadening and intensifying of religious life while the secular spirit took root.

The broadly secular society is relatively modern. (The term is used here to denote the growth of scientific skepticism rather than mere disbelief, or falling away, which has troubled the church through all ages.) Rational skepticism was much more pervasive among the early litterateurs than among the mass of men. The *philosophes*, and the great French Revolution they triggered, jolted religious orthodoxy, but by no means divorced the mass of men from their faith. The abandonment of religion is more recent, and is the result of a whole congeries of events, including the rise of science, critical analysis of Scripture, Darwinism, man's liberation from disease, the advent of technology and industry, mass populations, and not least, the abdication of the clergy. Broad secularism is, in fact, a twentieth-century phenomenon, even though its roots run back to the intellectual salons of past epochs. The flowering of skepticism is only just beginning. Madalyn Murray O'Hair is no historical accident, nor is her struggle to demote the church to a status beneath the omnicompetent state.

But neither is Mrs. O'Hair typical. For, in fact, most secular men do not consciously joust with religion the way she does, nor Robert G. Ingersoll did: they are not blazing atheists. Rather, most are agnostics who simply abandoned the church as irrelevant except perhaps at death. They find they can live reasonably pleasant and even exalted lives without bothering with the pews on Sunday, or prayer, or learning scriptural lessons, or communing with God. The bustling twentieth century is more interesting and relevant: there are stock markets to exploit, football, golf, corporate ladders, trips to exotic places, politics, sex, business deals, family vacations, records, and TV. Even moral ideals have simply been drained of their religious content. (Don't get pregnant, daughter: what would the neighbors

13

think?) Among the great mass of secular men the proposition that moral strictures must be obeyed because they come from God would be deemed bizarre. Religion has been sidetracked, like ancient railroad coaches rusting to death.

George Santayana was profoundly aware of the declining stature of religion when he wrote *The Last Puritan* in 1935. His hero, Oliver, struggles manfully with the proud Puritan heritage of his fathers which had become an irrelevant relic in the twentieth century. Just before Oliver dies in World War I, he sums up the desperation of his brittle faith—and, indeed, all religion—in the marching era of science.

> "I was born old," he says. "It is a dreadful inheritance, this of mine, that I need to be honest, that I need to be true, that I need to be just. That's not the fashion of today. The world is full of conscript minds, only they are in different armies, and nobody is fighting to be free, but each to make his own conscription universal. I can't catch the contagion. . . .

> "I was born a moral aristocrat, able to obey the voice of God, which means that of my own heart. My people first went to America as exiles into a stark wilderness to lead a life apart, purer and soberer, than the carnival life of Christendom. We were not content to be well dressed animals, rough or cunning or lustfully prowling or acquisitive, and perhaps inventing a religion to encourage us in our animality. We will not now sacrifice to Baal because we seem to have failed. We will bide our time. We will lie low and dip under, until the flood has passed and wasted itself over our heads. We are not wanted. In the world today we are a belated phenomenon, like April snow. Perhaps it is time for us to die. If we resist; if we try to cling to the fringes, as I have done so far, we are shaken off rudely, or allowed to hang on neglected or disowned."

Santayana's description of a Puritan clinging unwanted to the fringe of society is apt, and describes as well the status of Christianity now. The compromising church, both Roman and Protestant, waxes fat in the secular world and even exudes a saintliness while it toys with "post-Christian" ideals based primarily on the structural reform of society and government. The compromising church is popular in a sense, even among the swinging young who fill cathedrals with acid rock and sensual folk songs, and who yawn before the altar of God. But that other church clings to the fringes.

14

At no time in western history has the triangular confrontation between Christ's church, the state, and masses of people been more complex. On the eve of widespread collapse of the church's moral and religious authority in the nineteenth century, the church succeeded in embedding its moral codes deep into secular law. If the church was dying under the impact of Charles Darwin's discoveries, it at least intended to salvage its moral codes by incorporating them in public law. In particular, the church's codes of sexual conduct were injected into the law of countless communities. Thus the state became the handmaiden of the church, enforcing through coercion what was no longer enforceable through the church's own evanescing authority. This moral tenet was imposed far beyond the church's communicants and fell, one way or another, on nearly everyone. The rationale was that this was the law and will of God, and thus valid not merely for Christians, but for all.

Thus, in the nineteenth and the the early twentieth centuries, Christian codes were transferred almost in toto to units of government. The Sabbath commandment was the basis for a variety of Sunday blue laws, and these fell on all citizens, including Jews, agnostics, and Seventh Day Adventists. Its codes of sexual conduct were transformed into laws requiring marriage licenses and prohibiting adultery, sodomy, fornication, lewd behavior, pornography, and prostitution. A Protestant emphasis on sobriety became the rationale for Prohibition. Methodist opposition to gambling was codified into state law. Baptist opposition to dancing wended its way into law. What was good for Baptists or Methodists or Roman Catholics was deemed good for all men.

With Darwinism undermining the teachings and authority of the church, and with science explaining life's mysteries in terms of natural law, the retreating church in the nineteenth century plunged into the arms of the state not only in the United States, but in much of Europe as well. In England Victorianism triumphed as a ritual social expression of the church's rejection of carnality. In America, the drive to codify church law in government reached its apex in Prohibition, and then waned rapidly under the impact of modern secularism. In a breathtakingly brief period, mainly since World War II, the whole legal apparatus to enforce morals collapsed. Only a couple of decades ago hotel dicks prowled the halls looking for adulterers. Only two decades ago, cops locked up people for fornication, carnal knowledge, sodomy, and other infractions of church-made law. Now they are all dead letters, except perhaps in the South. Prohibition is demolished. Drug abuse laws are enforced mainly in the breach. Laws pertaining to property are undermined on the secular proposition that society is at fault for permitting unequal wealth. Blue laws are wiped out.

Most sexual conduct is now explicitly protected by the courts. This demolition was achieved in less than half a century, beginning with the revulsion toward Prohibition. And in the process, there also collapsed the notion that human character could be reformed and edified by public law.

It is noteworthy that the waning church's effort to use the state as its life raft collapsed totally and rapidly. The state is not a source of moral authority, and it was unnatural for it to enforce moral codes that depend, at bottom, on conscience and voluntary acceptance. The state, moreover, is subject to democratic process. If secular men wish to torpedo any of the blue laws, they can and do press for abolition. Thus, the state is always a poor repository for church law. The embodiment of church codes in state law is not normal in Western civilization. In most circumstances, moral infractions have been handled by ecclesiastical courts rather than civil or criminal ones. Things routinely outlawed now, such as prostitution, were usually brought before the bar of bishops rather than the bar of kings.

The church may be faulted for overreaching; for attempting to combat skepticism by coercing the appearance of outward Christianity. That overreach was pathetic, because it denied the most fundamental of Christian doctrines: that those who reach toward God must do so out of their own volition, freely, through conviction and faith. The problem churches face in the future is not only the obliteration of authority, but the continuing reaction of secular men to the church's excess zeal. A disintegrated Christianity still informs men of right and wrong—to a degree. But ultimately, secular progressives must question the validity of even the residual Christian heritage.

The recent Christian response has been to rally around the remaining moral codes embedded in law—but this may be tragically short-sighted inasmuch as religion ought not to be under the purview of secular authorities. So upside down is this epoch that even antistatist conservatives whose libertarian programs call for liquidating the New Deal and all its welfarist successors are rushing to defend the majesty and authority of state moral law against the nihilism of the left. That defense is mounted not without pain, inasmuch as the libertarians of the right are splitting away from the mainstream conservatives to retain their traditional enmity toward all government. The splintering of the right will probably increase, rather than decrease, as the secular left becomes more militant in its revolutionary aims. It is becoming more and more difficult to advocate any sort of libertarian reform—such as reducing the size and authority of the federal government—when woolly revolutionaries are burning down the house. To propose specific diminutions of state authority in such a topsy-turvy situation is to side with the revolutionaries in a tactical sense, no matter how abhorrent revolution is to those on the right. This does not mean that conservatives are backing themselves into a pro-government corner. For if bloated government is to be deflated in a revolutionary era, some pressure must be brought against berserk bureaucracy as well as berserk radicals. But that force ought not be be political. Rather, it should be moral and spiritual, and should stem from a newly vitalized church. The pneumatic government and the pneumatic revolutionaries are not expressions of excessive authority, but rather expressions of its absence. The bureaucracy balloons into the vacuum left by retreating authority. Were the church able to assume its proper magisterium, and were the state able to command its proper allegiance, there would be neither gross bureaucracies, nor armies of revolutionaries. Perhaps the church cannot reassert its transcendent authority without a divine event to electrify the world anew. But at least it ought to be clear that the church, rather than government, is the one avenue toward domestic peace. All government can do is repress or compel outward conformity. But the church can convert the rebellious; it can turn dissent into assent.

There exists in what was once called Christendom an uncompromising Christian remnant. It is a small fraction of those who are nominally religious. The remnant will not yield to the secular world and is therefore more truly radical in these times than any secular leftist radical ever dreamed of being. The remnant will not bow to moral decay, or demythologized religion, or an abstract God. It will be resented principally by the apostate factions of the church. The question faced by the remnant is whether this is to be a Christian civilization, or whether Christianity is to be merely a sect within a secular civilization. If the latter, then a variety of public laws that invade personal liberty insofar as secular men are concerned would have to be repealed and the remnant would be forced to live in a modern Gomorrah.

Theoretically it would be possible for a Christian to maintain his faith and morals in Gomorrah, but in actuality that would be difficult. The libertarian argument is that religion is voluntary, and not something to be imposed on others. However, this view treats religion as merely another "ism" competing in the market of ideas. It is no such thing. It is an overarching moral and spiritual authority, and for believers, divinely ordained. It is difficult, if not impossible, for a Christian who may oppose, say, abortion, not to feel that the state is countenancing murder if it permits feticide. It is his *political* right in a democracy to favor laws against abortion, even as it is the political right of secular men to try to liberalize the law. Conversely, the militant secularist might find reasons to invade some of Christianity's sacred practices. He might, on public health grounds, for example,

17

oppose the communal communion chalice. He, likewise, has the democratic right to pursue his reform. But if he does, he is confronting not merely the practice of another "ism" but belief and faith of a transcendent nature, and is likely to meet outrage. There cannot be, I am suggesting, a routine marketplace of ideas where religion is concerned. The emperors of Rome sought to incorporate Christianity into the empire's pantheistic paganism. It didn't work because Christians cannot compromise. Persecutions failed to dim the torch of the new faith. Thus, the glib formula of the libertarian stumbles upon the unique intransigence of Christianity.

The deepening strife between religious and secular men is expressed not only directly in theological debate but also, to a large measure, in the liberal-conservative cockfight, and now most especially in the conflict of the generations. The hip kids and the young radicals are unalloyed secularists—except for the Jesus freaks—and they are expressing flamboyant skepticism of the residual religion of their elders. The alienated kids are, of course, a minority of their peers, but they are at the center of a generation's thinking. While perhaps a majority of the young people are not openly or expressly hip, they borrow heavily from the alienated ones. The language, the clothing, the ornaments of the flower children have been widely copied. The political manifestoes of the young radicals, slightly diluted, occupy innumerable others who stay more or less within the system. The alienated kids are thus important beyond their numbers as the seedstock of a naturalist secularism. They are natural men: a generation trying to discard guilt, the fetters of the past, and the fogeyish codes of faith. They are the secret *beau ideal* of aging liberals who have yearned for years to discard the shackles. They are, for many liberals, the greening of America. The various kid cults all have their own emphases, but in this book they will be treated as a unified phenomenon: the dropouts, the flower children, the pharmaceuticals, and acid-rock addicts will be treated in common with the Yippies and Weathermen as part of a secularist impulse that is rapidly stripping away the last of religious orthodoxy in America. It is noteworthy that Pope Paul dwells at length on messages to the young, especially the carnal young. For there is everywhere in traditional Christianity the understanding that the kids and their counterculture form a radical break with the faith, and even with the history of the West. To be sure, the hip kids adopt some of the ideals of Christianity, and some of the goodness that is universalized in all the great faiths of man. But they also have accepted into their codes some explicitly anti-Christian things, such as free sexuality and situation ethics.

The intent here is to discuss the gulf between secular and religious men in America, and to dwell on the social implications of the struggle. The kids and their counterculture will be particularly emphasized because the kids are extirpating the established order with breathtaking ease. They are moving so rapidly against only recently hallowed things that one can only surmise that most of America's beliefs and values are decayed, and that the timbers of the Establishment are riddled with termites and are crumbling. The church has long since ceased to restore the rotted beams; indeed, the church has pretty much decamped to the counterculture. That is what this book is about. It is about the *kids*, especially, who won't recognize themselves at all on these pages.

2. CHRISTIANITY AND REPRESSION

THERE is no doubt in the minds of New Leftists, and secularists in general, that Christianity is highly repressive, especially when allied with the coercive engine of government. Herbert Marcuse and others have fulminated against a society they believe so constraining and dehumanizing that no man has the freedom to achieve any self-realization. This viewpoint seems incredible to those of us who find freedom everywhere to become what we wish and do what we want—but set that aside for the nonce. Marcuse holds that a militarist elite prospers by heavily suppressing the aspiration of the great mass of people, particularly disfranchised minorities, and that only a continuing leftward revolution will liberate those masses of men who are de facto slaves of opulent warlords. Marcuse goes so far as to suggest that the just society will be weighted to repress rightist forces, but will be totally tolerant of any movement from the left, that is, any force that further democratizes government, removes coercions, and abolishes tradition and authority such as that of the church. Marcuse's rationalization of repression of the right with a libertarian, liberating society *for all* reveals a glaring inconsistency. Yet, paradoxically, he asserts that he does not favor an elitist dictatorship of the left that will decide what's antisocial.

Marcuse's dialectics are a radicalized version of traditional liberalism.

The enemies are the same: the right wing, conservatism, tradition, authority, religion. The ultimate target of Marcuse's New Left as well as the secular liberals is the church, the giver of norms and standards of right conduct, and the deposit of authority based on revelation. The church is the sole remaining structure in nihilistic twentieth-century society that summons awe and veneration; the sole force that evokes conscience, guilt, and a sense of wrongdoing. These are what Marcuse and his New Leftists hate most of all. Guilt is, in his estimation, a cruel internalized punishment for conduct that is usually, in his estimation, perfectly innocent and acceptable.

The dilemma of Marcusian dialectics is that, in Edmund Burke's phrase, there must be checks placed on human appetites at some point, and if they are not within, then they must be imposed from without. Burke's implication is that a society of guiltless unfettered men is one ungovernable, or at least governed only by a tyrant. Perhaps this is what inspired St. Paul to write in Corinthians, "where the spirit of the Lord is, there is liberty."

Not only the New Left, but also the secular-liberal "respectable" left as well, fails to understand the role of Christianity as the keystone of human liberty; indeed as the reason western societies have generally permitted infinitely more freedom and individuality than the tradition-oriented and authoritarian societies of the Orient.

Traditional Christianity, rooted in Judaism, is the fountain of individuality. The entire New Testament is a manual of private conduct: how one should behave toward God; toward fellow man, neighbors, family, and even enemies. There is not a single instance in Matthew, Mark, Luke, or John, of Jesus proposing structural reform of the social order: no social security, no public welfare, no seditious uprising against the Romans; no minimum wage; no child labor laws; no coerced redistribution of income. Nothing. What does exist is a heavy stress on the inward personality. Moral and ethical standards—mainly "Thou Shalt Nots"—are established as the negative ideal for individuals. There are things to shun, things that are done only on pain of guilt and shame. To the extent that each Christian communicant internalizes these standards, self-governing and self-governed man is by definition free. Guilt, conscience, agonizing personal appraisal of one's own conduct—these are the tools and gifts of free men, the means by which state control is rendered superfluous.

Likewise, there are positive standards embodied in the great commandment to love God and "thy neighbor as thyself." And there are endless admonitions to love and be concerned, and be voluntarily a good Samaritan in all human endeavor. All these positive standards were repeatedly urged upon Christians from the beginning, not as some prescription for others, or

22

some one *else* or "society," or "the nation"—but as codes of conduct for each listener, for each person who came into contact with the teachings of the Master. It was only by internalizing these great codes, Jesus explained, that a person could achieve salvation: first through faith in Him and his divine mission, and second, through adhering personally to these codes even through adversity.

To be sure, certain conduct was forbidden: extramarital sex for example, along with murder, cheating, lying, and envy. And a certain behavior is required, including observance of the sabbath, charity, brotherhood, mercy, and generosity. All these, in a sense, delimit freedom. A man arrested for adultery, after all, is a man denied the right to practice adultery. But are these rights and are they freedoms? At least in the scriptural sense, most of the proscribed activity is a species of enslavement of mind and body to base passions that prevent the fulfillment of personality and the liberation of mind and spirit. In the Christian viewpoint, the proscribed activities imprison a man. God is guiding those who love him not toward a massive restraint on conduct, but toward an unfettered spirit. God's yoke is light, not heavy, Jesus explained.

The New Testament also injects love into the law of God, and this, too, appears at first to infringe on the liberty of men to do as they choose, live as selfishly as they choose, or be as mean as they choose. Love, however, is described as the fulfillment of the old Hebraic law. Where before men obeyed the law because they were constrained to do so, henceforth they would, through love, fulfill the law because they want to. This, then, is a thrust toward liberty, rather than away from it. Laws can chafe and chain the heart, but a deep love for others does not.

If love were as fully practiced as prescribed by Christ, the need for most of the coercions of the welfare state would wither away. The welfare state is not an example of social success, but of public failure. Any instance in which coercion must be used to fulfill responsibilities that free men fail to meet must be regarded as a failure. The welfare state is grounded on coerced giving: tax money is extracted from those able to pay regardless of whether they approve of how it is spent, and then distributed to the needy. The fact that some taxpayers are glad to see their taxes used for charitable ends in no way alters the coercive nature of the arrangement. Obviously a system of voluntary giving to those in need would come much closer to the Christian ideal, so long as the needs of the poor were actually met. Enough people have given rein to their greed and envy, forgetting their Christian obligations to their fellows, to trigger an expanding welfare state. Taxes are the means by which they are forced to care for others, and taxes are coercive. To destroy a man's liberty entirely, it is only necessary to tax

23

away his income. The point of all this is clear: Christianity is a libertarian force, and not a repressive one. The harder people try, through love, to care for others and govern their own passions, the freer they may be; and the less necessary is the omnicompetent state. The church did try hard and nobly to care for those in trouble. The system of hospitals established throughout America by churches is one of religion's more impressive monuments. Many of those hospitals, even now, are staffed with virtually unpaid help: nursing nuns who by aiding those in distress serve their Master. When tallying the pluses and minuses of human liberty, it would be wise to consider the church's manifold charities, and then consider the burden in public taxes, out of our own pockets, that would be needed to replace these good works. Even now, in its vexed and waning days, the church operates vast charitable enterprises including hospitals, day care centers, orphanages, schools, colleges, old people's homes, rest homes, ghetto medical clinics, and havens for girls in distress. Their contribution to human liberty—both in terms of taxes saved and responsibilities fulfilled—is incalculable.

From this a reasonably sound generalization can be discerned: Judeo-Christian love is the source of great liberty. Because some people care, and even surrender whole lives to caring, the welfare states of most nations don't reach coercive and totalitarian levels. The New Left will not wreck the church, but if hypothetically it should, it could supply no mechanism for charity and freedom that equals the church, and in the end would fall back on the state to succor the needy and crush ungovernable citizens.

Human liberty is not absolute. If all the mechanisms of self-government were removed from the soul, man would have no compunctions about murdering, lying, cheating, stealing, brutalizing, cursing, and raping. The very forces Marcuse and his colleagues deplore in western societies are really the governing mechanisms that enable us to control our private selves. We learn to feel guilty. We learn embarrassment, shame, sorrow, and the joy of giving to others and caring for others. We learn to repent our daily transgressions. We become fine-tuned instruments of awareness of the rights and needs of others. To the extent we fail to internalize these social mechanisms, the state forces us to. The terrible aspect of New Left ideology and all the post-Freudian claptrap is not merely that it numbs the conscience, but that it assails every standard, every norm. It does not seek merely to free individuals from the allegedly repressive impact of an evanescent Christian moral and ethical system; it attacks the system itself by shocking it into callousness. Hence, the public nudity, obscenity, and errant violence. To be sure, the New Left has a few values. Before the bombers bomb, they call to evacuate the building, which suggests

24

somewhat more reverence for life than the turn-of-the-century anarchists who bombed to kill. But one wonders how long even some reverence for life will persist in those who are straining against every vestigial remnant of moral order? It is truly impossible to assault morals and ethics without simultaneously undermining liberty.

Even in the realm of custom, courtesy, and everyday civility, all of which have little immanent moral or ethical importance, there are pillars of liberty that ought not to be destroyed by the first barbarian wandering along the alley. For generations Christendom has painfully erected customs—or manners if you will—aimed to assuage the angry heart, relax the fearful, pacify the aggressive, and tame the violent. We use courtesy in addressing strangers: that is, in addressing people whose inner passions we do not yet understand. We separate acquaintances from friends. We use simple expressions of gratitude a hundred times daily to express appreciation for services rendered. We signal our need for a favor, or help, with a prefatory Please. We dress in ways we hope will not offend. We recognize a certain fitness of conduct, such as not wearing twin-holstered pistols and a cartridge belt while strolling down Fifth Avenue. We make small judgments about the humans we come into contact with. All this, in New Left ideology, is part of the repressive burden that enslaved persons must bulldoze away. But in fact, it is part of the brick and mortar of human liberty. If the New Left succeeds in dynamiting common civility, it will divest people of all those sensitive testing mechanisms with which we feel each other out and remove menace. It is a part of Jerry Rubin's militant game to shock assemblages by having a nude girl deliver a pig on a platter to a speaker, or by drowning out a speaker with the most provocative sexual obscenities, or by appearing at public hearings in outlandish garb meant to strip the proceedings of all dignity and authority. All these activities may appear at first blush to be exercises in liberty. However, their intent is to shred manners and customs, and to awaken a sense of menace in the unwilling spectators. Human liberty is grounded in trust. We are largely free to do as we will because we are trusted. Our government trusts us; our peers trust us. We are trusted a thousand ways every day, not only in the obvious way, such as when cashing a check, but in the obscure ways. We trust the receptionist we hire won't suddenly rise up and club some stranger. We trust the milkman won't throw milk cartons at the side of the house. We trust the people we invited for dessert and bridge won't steal the silver. If we did not trust, there could be little liberty because the state would have to replace trust with guns. In the Orient as well as the Occident, there are elaborate codifications of conduct designed to smooth over human relationships, and these codes usually help mitigate the powers

25

of tyrants and dictators. We witnessed in the American Revolution the survival, virtually intact, of social mores and morals as well as English common law. But in the French Revolution, the social and religious as well as political fabric was shredded, with the result that France was engulfed in new tyrannies and tumults for generations, while the United States quickly developed into the freest society on earth.

The New Left is flirting with the notion that there should be neither inward nor outward restraints on human behavior. The Marcusian dialectic is filled with the Freudian notion of expelling guilt or other ''repression'' from the inward self. Much of the remainder of his opaque doctrine is a diatribe built around a Marxist analysis of class war. The hippie golden rule, ''do your thing but don't hurt others,'' comes as close to a codification of conduct as anything existing in the youth movement. The flower children, to the extent their codes are not a put-on, subscribe to a mushy code based more on dropping out than on any altruism. On the other hand, the political New Left's version of liberty is as totalist and simplistic as its analysis of the ills of America—and as false. The idea of a society without restraints, without authority, ought to be called what it is: depravity. The idea that the destruction of authority will usher in an era of flower children is grotesque. Even now, flower children populate our asylums and prisons and welfare rolls because they cannot cope with their own passions, or cope with the *freedom* of the civilized, Christianized world.

In fact, the whole youth cult could properly be classified as a phenomenon of young people terrified by the vast liberty of a permissive society. Their public and private conduct is producing not more freedom, but more restraint everywhere in the Republic. The fear of liberty runs so deep in some of them that they cop out entirely into the drug culture, or madness. They are aware they have an opportunity unique in the history of man to become anything they choose, to go as far as their wits will carry them, and that is a frightening prospect, especially for those so ill-disciplined that they have never acquired inner character. Even the sex cults, the shacking up, the sexual freedom leagues, are really an escape from the unbearable liberty available to the young of America and much of Europe. Because these kids have so little toughness or character or resilience they are distressed by a society that says: run as far as you can with all your resources. The cop-outs don't want to run, and don't want to live with the self-condemnation of failure, either, or with the scorn of the successful falling on their heads.

Liberty terrifies Herbert Marcuse. It terrifies the New Left. It appalls Tom Hayden and Mark Rudd. It drove Timothy Leary out of this world. It scares the Jefferson Airplane and the Rolling Stones, and Angela Davis.

For those unprepared for it, liberty is the most frightful bomb ever to explode on the human psyche. If by their fruits we shall know them, the youth cults are guilty of provoking more government repression than any groups in our history. The kids want to shrink freedom to a safe dimension, to a world of rules that is comfortable and acceptable for their weak-kneed selves. Thanks to the antics of the youth cults, there are now on the books a variety of ill-advised proto-police state laws that menace the entire citizenry.

The kids sometimes appear to be testing the limits of parental tolerance. They loathe that tolerance, and our anything-goes society. They loathe the permissiveness with which they were reared, and regard it properly as a mark of parental unconcern. There's no love in permissiveness. Discipline is a component of parental love, and no one knows that better than the undisciplined child who must find out the hard way—by constant testing of society—what the requirements are for mature adulthood. The kids are testing and failing to find frontiers of resistance from their elders. Their testing turns to contempt and hatred for a society so spongy that it has lost its values. It is no wonder the totalitarian societies catch their fancy; no wonder they play at revolution with impunity, the way previous generations played at politics. The only authentic frontiers they have discovered to date are bombing and hijacking which meet with swift and harsh social retaliation.

The reason Herbert Marcuse is the guru of the New Left and the kid cults is not that he is an authentic libertarian—though he prattles endlessly about repression—but because his is a formula for comforting government control. If Marcuse were an authentic libertarian he would scarcely be advocating a maximized state with social or governmental ownership of production. He is remarkably silent when it comes to economic liberty, or laissez faire, without which social and personal liberties are unlikely to evolve very far. He has all sorts of instincts to control others: he hates overpopulation and pollution, each of which require massive regimentation. He hates the right wing and proposes controls for it. He hates religion and seems to favor outlawing it or driving it underground. All this is scarcely the freedom-cry of a libertarian, but rather a garden-variety statist, whose hatred of the state exists only so long as the *other* side controls it. No, the reason he is so popular with the young, along with behaviorial psychologist B. F. Skinner, is because he wants to narrow the area of free conduct, even as Skinner seeks to narrow our sense of responsibility.

Perhaps it is presumptuous to argue that at some level the kid cults reject freedom and long for a society with more boundaries. It is, after all, in the name of freedom (and peace!) that most campus uproars are initiated.

27

For the sake of peace and freedom, people's parks are stormed, the draft is opposed, drug and sex laws abominated, and ghetto life resisted. The most authentic yearnings for liberty rest within the blacks who in any case are part of the New Left for different and more valid reasons than any middle-class white kids.

The white kids inherit from their liberal mentors an ambiguity about freedom. A liberal civil libertarian is zealous about certain liberties within a narrow range having to do with communications, but is usually the rankest state interventionist when it comes to economic practice, or property ownership. In the realms of consumerism and pollution control there is a new thrust toward state domination, on top of older liberal thrusts toward statist charity and controls over working conditions, wages, monopoly, utility ownership, etc. In fact, until very recently liberals maintained a veritable love affair with government, and especially with the executive branch. One can turn to old copies of the *Congressional Record* and discover Hubert Humphrey orating about the good works of government, about Peace Corps and VISTAs, about all that would flow from this or that public program if only the government would tax and spend more. It is axiomatic, however, that a government that taxes highly and intrudes deeply lessens the range of liberty. This willingness to accept such intrusions in economic life has been inherited intact by the kid cults with the exception that some of the kids have learned to hate the bureaucracies, though not the social goals of the bureaus.

Thus, we find a curious ambivalence shredding the whole youth movement. The kids complain of repression and point readily to rough cops, drug busts, and so on. Yet, a truly libertarian world is unthinkable to them. Senator Goldwater's general objective to cut taxes and the size of the federal establishment in half—a true libertarian prescription—is unthinkable and fascist (never mind that fascists were statists who sought to incorporate all endeavor into the life of the party and state).

Is it being suggested, then, that the kid cults don't really feel repressed? No. They feel unfree, and in fact they do lack freedom in some ways. The argument here is that their sense of confinement stems not so much from any tyrannical institutions, but from their own weakness and inability to master their own unruly selves. Their oppression stems from their failure to mature into adults. They are, in the last analysis, a miserably undisciplined generation, lacking patience and routine perseverance; seeking instant solutions to stubborn problems. To the extent that the kids cannot marshal their inner resources and direct them toward achievement, they naturally feel oppressed from without. They feel oppressed, but do not discern the nature of that oppression. Their literature and art express the weakness. Their literature is childish, garish, and undisciplined. Their music is unstructured and simple and noisy, rather than melodic and gracious. They are frequently bright but there is no way for them to direct their brilliance into fruitful enterprise. They scorn their parents' material abundance but not particularly because they are spartans. Rather, they scorn what they are incapable of acquiring because they are too weak to gather the goods of this earth around them. The perpetual students, or semistudents, or campus street people, are saying something about themselves and the cosy academic womb they cling to. Given funds, they are anything but ascetic. Given riches, they are the crassest materialists.

Their lack of morals is in itself an oppressive facet of their lives. Somewhere within them they know there must be boundaries on human conduct. You do not routinely murder thy neighbor. But they live in a liberal milieu which refuses to recognize or enforce boundaries; a world of amiable campus presidents who offer tea and sympathy—but no crackdowns. A world of faculty members who are engaged in jousting with the world themselves and have a wide streak of sympathy for any longhair who is discovered in a basket on their front stoop. Freedom is not even definable until social boundaries are ascertained. When the kids can't locate the boundaries, they are faced with the dilemma of establishing or assuming attitudes within society that may or may not really exist. They see repression everywhere, in short, because they can't locate where freedom ends. This is manifest in their quaint, curious attacks on shopworn devils.

Character is definable not only as right conduct but as inner strength. The lack of character means a life lost to intense frustration, hunger, lovelessness, and stasis. For the weak, even the freest societies are oppressive. To a petulant, childish, unregulated person, the whole world seems to conspire to crush all the little flowers of hope and love. The kids rationalize their weakness, of course: the guitar-strumming bearded bards are evoked as a new "life style" superior to the old slaves of material progress. But curiously, those "slaves" never felt enslaved. Indeed, their rising incomes and mobility enabled them to discover new plateaus of life in travel, the arts, business, and hospitality that were undreamed of by men through all of history. There is scarcely a city of consequence without its little theater, painting club, travel group, sportsmen's association, etc. And this is to suggest only the organized aspects of free society. There are countless thousands who pursue their interests unfettered. They are the empirical evidence of enduring liberty.

3. VERSIONS OF SALVATION

THE kids still believe in the faltering strength of science and the weakness of God. Science solves things and makes things go. God doesn't seem to solve anything. Science hurtles men to the moon, conquers disease, transplants organs, makes plastics, synthesizes protoplasm, runs industries, and conquers nature. God seems to be holed up in his corner of the universe sulking.

Science could also, in the eyes of the young, provide rational solutions to all the social problems. Behaviorists such as B. F. Skinner, who is also a guru of the New Left, hold out the possibility that man will be able to weed out sorrows and emerge breathlessly into a utopia of love, peace, and order. Science will somehow not only feed the poor but destroy their envy; it will fill the emptiness and boredom of existence with computerized, guaranteed excitement.

Faith in science is the last, flickering hope of both kids and liberals. Science is now broadly defined as the quest for knowledge, tested empirically. If it works, man has advanced to a new plateau. Ultimately with all knowledge science can heal all things, and the gods of the earth will not need the God of heaven. Even morals will ultimately be tested and rejected or upheld by sound scientific evidence rather than flimsy faith or tradition.

The Fabians were among the first to seek scientific solutions to man's sorrows. If science provided the blueprint, the state would provide the engine of social well-being. The same attitude runs deep through American liberalism to this day, and social engineering has become the principal route to salvation. Social engineering is the conscious manipulation of environmental factors—such as slums or classrooms or the structure of government—and if it is done right, benefits should accrue to the poor and helpless. Social engineering is believed to be the solution for everything from racism to loneliness and guilt. It is the central credo of liberalism. The state is the engine of liberalism even though civil libertarians distrust certain (but not all) statist activities. If science is the godhead of secular liberalism—all-powerful and all-knowing—then the state is liberalism's Jesus Christ, the route to redemption and salvation, the Way to Terrestrial Paradise. Science illumines what Eric Voegelin calls the gnostic heresy, the erection of a utopia on earth through meliorist human effort.

Over against science is God the Forgotten, the Creator, the Comforter, the Everlasting Father, the Lord, and King of Kings. Such an evocation of power and glory is simply puzzling, if not embarrassing to secular men, and especially the young ones who accept the wonders of science—jets, TV, H-bombs, heart transplants, etc.—with total aplomb as the natural status of man. In their eyes Almighty God is not almighty. Through Old and New Testaments the strength and power of God runs as a litany. He shall break His enemies with a rod of iron; with Him all things are possible; He shall move mountains. He created the universe out of His substance, and the fishes and birds and insects and animals, and then He created man.

All this is fancy; lyrical, perhaps, but unreal now. Science, and not God, reigneth on high. Even among Christians, God has paled to a capricious, impotent benefactor rather than Lord of Lords and King of Kings. And that is understandable enough when we think how often prayer seems to avail not at all, while penicillin accomplishes everything. When an injection seems to cure what even the terrible power of God seems not to heal, then it is scarcely surprising that the vision of an omnipotent God is drained and deflated. All the majestic symbolism of the Bible—that we are sheep and He is our shepherd, for example—loses its power when the penicillin-shepherd gathers us to a safety that the God-shepherd couldn't or wouldn't lead us to. Where is the rod and staff to comfort us? Better that we trust in the rod and staff of science and government to tell us what sort of proteins and vitamins we need, or how we shall redistribute incomes to aid the needy. Better the rod of the state to administer justice along more tolerant lines than the impossible justice of God. Man is more merciful than God. Man forgives; God casts into hell. Man's justice is freer and fairer.

32

All this consideration, all this science-oriented salvation, then, has reduced the Lord of Lord and King of Kings to a marginal existence on the fringe of human society. The roles are reversed: we are the lords of the universe and God, if He exists, is the servant, the power to be resorted to only after our science founders, and our knowledge is up against a (temporary) barrier. Man has his foot on the neck of God.

A sensitive few remember the older cosmology, perhaps when hearing the thunderous evocation of God's power in the Hallelujah chorus at Eastertide, or perhaps in the quiet of their prayers when closeted away from the secular floods. Some don't doubt that God rules, that every sparrow is still counted, and every hair on every head is still numbered, and every commandment still applies, and that He ultimately breaks proud men with a rod of iron, but calls His sons and daughters to Him in love. Some remember God, and remember to kneel in all humility and awe in the presence of the Shepherd. But these are the dwindling remnant and their version of salvation has been beached on the shores of history and buried beneath the sands of time. Now that man has the very power of the sun at hand, he can remake the universe to suit his needs and the Lord of Creation can be safely interred in the crypts of mythology.

The Fabians and liberals had, at least, a scheme of salvation in the benevolent and omnipotent state: more medicare, social security, welfare, higher taxes, protection of unions, higher minimum wages—all these and more in extensive catalogues of reform. This was the avenue toward a good and just order informed by a liberal moral vision.

The kids are less certain about that secular utopia than their liberal elders. The godhead state also drafts kids for Vietnam-type wars, builds hydrogen bombs and rockets, extracts suffocating taxes, and busts their pot parties. If the liberals were ambivalent about their secular godhead, the kids are even more so. The kids are inclined to reject all the cosmologies—the statist, scientific, and secular ones as well as the ancient Christian one. In fact, the horror in the heart of so many of the kids—the radicals especially—is that there is no salvation and therefore no hope. It is the certitude that no redemption of any sort exists that lies darkly in the heart of each radical. For ultimately, if there is no salvation, there is no worth, not even in historic beliefs and things. It is significant that the bombers have chosen mainly government, business, and academic edifices to bomb, and rarely the church. They are dynamiting that with the least potential for salvation—and coincidentally that which is most liberal and secular. But they hate the churches too, and the houses of the Lord may someday receive their share of dynamite. The wild young are not radicalized by a terrible past, but rather a horrible future without redemption. It is not historic hurts (except for some minorities) which motivate the young radicals. It is the anguished prospect of life without hope and comfort; it is the failure of the vision of the state as godhead that still grips the middle-class liberals. It is the rejection of the Christian cosmology and the redemption offered by Jesus Christ. It is more than frightening, more than desperate to them that they can find no institution that proffers hope.

Somewhere along the line in recent years the vision of Progress has ground to a halt. The idea that man is marching ineluctably leftward and upward—the old progressivism—is suddenly embarrassing in an epoch of advancing barbarity and chaos. Yet progress as recently as a decade ago was a cardinal tenet of leftist thought. Liberals still hoped and believed that "programs" would ameliorate distress and build a more humane and peaceful society. They feel cheated now, and blame devils, such as business or Republicans or militarists for the shocking collapse and inadequacy of most established programs such as the war on poverty or urban renewal. And no bigger devil wrestled against Progress than the Vietnam war, even though the total expenditure on it had declined to a relatively insignificant part of the whole federal budget. But a handy devil it was to explain away the collapse of order in the United States and the deepening awareness that there is not forward movement, but rather decay, regression, retreat, and disunity after nearly four decades of massive liberalistic interventions in the economy and society. Progress today has an ironic ring about it, and those who use the word inject a sardonic awareness of the inexorable march into hell. Pitiful progressives! The very word reeks of an older optimism, an orthodoxy of the left that stumbles now to the tune of an uncertain trumpet, and advances its programs as ritual, to sustain the flagging hope that they are still marching toward terrestrial paradise. Not even that prototype progressive and gabby optimist Hubert Humphrey sounds the bells for progress now: the whole nation is absorbed with greater enterprises such as minimizing damage, and marshaling some small resistance to the galloping disintegration at every hand.

The conservative criticisms of progressive legislation have been scornful and pungent. The "progress" of urban renewal has been to wipe out thousands of low-rent housing units. The "progress" of protected monopoly unionism has been to wipe out American products—and jobs—from countless world markets. The "progress" of the liberal clergy has been to demolish God, morals, and reverence. The kids know about the myth of progress, and that is why they hoot at politicians who ritually intone all the clichés of progress at the altar of the electorate. The kids would accept a moral and ethical cosmology if it could originate in pure science, leaving no room for doubt. Its provenance would be in the cold rationality of mathematics, and its faith would be pure empirical performance, and progress would be the residue of skeptical analysis.

The ritual obeisance to Progress, especially among venal politicians and bureaucrats, is part of a formula of politics that requires presidents and aldermen to worship at its altar. There is no such thing as progress, except in the minds of politicians. Improvements here and there, perhaps, but only against a tide of calamities and darkening hopes and flickering candle stubs. And the things that were once conquered now fester and multiply: the germs that penicillin once banished are back, in more resistant form. The hybrid grains we grow to feed the masses of men have less and less protein. The VD that was to disappear is now epidemic. Vanquished cholera now stalks the globe. It were as though God is reminding man that without Him there is no salvation; that man's puny devices to ease life could be dashed away in a moment, with God's rod of iron. Progress indeed, with the worms gutting the corpse of reform! If God is dead, His dead hand is deadening life and hope, and the reaper is everywhere.

The kids know it. And the terrible knowledge lies knotted in their bellies. But while they disbelieve the current myths of progress, they know there ought to be progress, and many cling desperately to the myth rather than accept the grimmer, starker possibility that man may be utterly incapable of working out his redemption unaided by God. That is why the future is unbearable to them, and why so many cop out and turn to a more primitive life in pioneer circumstances, out of touch with the "real" world.

It was hoped once that rising affluence would eradicate most social and moral evils. Material abundance was, in the liberal viewpoint, to have minimized theft, but the theory collapses now, with affluence and crime rising hand in hand, while the Great Depression emerges from the mists of time as a period of remarkable morality and honesty. It was also hoped that material abundance would solve multitudes of problems such as alcoholism, divorce, disease, derangement, etc., but it has done none of that. Indeed, materialism seems to be original sin: it fosters multiple evils. The kids know that, too, and seem ungrateful to their grubbing elders. But they are not ungrateful; rather, skeptical, and perhaps aware of the corruption of the spirit that material obsessions sometimes bring.

The ways of God are unsearchable, but there is the intuition in Christianity that heaven exists because there can be no salvation in worldly ways. That idea is almost unbearable to secular men, and especially to liberals whose vision of redemption ends on the misty shores of a good and just and loving society in which men are devoid of guilt. That vision is the *raison d'être* of the liberal Unitarian Church, whose members usually re-

35

ject afterlife and concentrate on reforming the here and now through government programs. The terrible thing about those hopeful programs is that they are ultimately doomed. Some progressives, upon seeing that each reform generates unanticipated new problems, lash out at devils such as bureaucrats who allegedly never administered the programs properly. But many liberals are too realistic for that and deep within are facing the sickening realization that the centralized benevolent state, or any structural tinkering of society, is a one-note rag with neither beginning nor end, and devoid of progress. Governments, at bottom, are bodies of organized monopolistic coercion, and the secular vision of using this appalling power founders upon the venality of those who are given such power. If there is no authority informing the governors, no God, no ethic, no morals, then the state is scarcely an instrument of salvation, and the "programs" become pure politics—the purchase, through subsidy, of allegiances and votes from client groups. The vision of progress founders, as well, on the habit of looking to some abstraction, such as "society" or "government" for solutions, instead of examining the individual self.

The other secular paths toward salvation are nearly as grim. Individualism—the doctrine of free, willful moral development by each person—is nobler than the statist liberal's ideal, but is wholly aristocratic. There will never be more than a handful of men capable of self-government; of wrestling with their passions so successfully that the need for the state would wither away. Individualism is a splendid ideal: in the breast of each participant there would be a commitment to self-improvement and integrity. The individualist ideal is surely superior to the liberal combination of self-indulgence and statist expansion. The individualist ideal is a part of a disintegrated puritanism: it focuses on a man's character and is, or was, informed by Christian ethics. But individualism prospered at the expense of community and common norms. The great nineteenth-century individualists smashed as they built, and if they scorned community feelings, they ultimately paved the way for the modern hippie individualism that also scorns community norms and is economically destructive and parasitic. Neither the disintegrated individualism of the kid cults nor the early individualism of the nineteenth-century industrial giants appears to be an ultimate road to salvation. To the extent that it ignored and offended the sensibilities and rights of others, it bred not peace and not love, but abrasiveness, plunder, and antagonism throughout the social structure. But in individualism lay great hope because it was a pathway to responsible man, who was to be free, whose actions were to be voluntary, and who was to build a social order based on contract. There are many, both liberal and conservative, who have loved the individualist vision, the

36

vision of free, responsible man in voluntary community. Among conservatives, in particular, there was hope of an individualism informed by the church; indeed, to some, individuality was a product of Christian emphasis on self-government. The earlier, or classical liberalism discarded the Christian restraints and tried to build an individualism based on total private freedom, but this vision quickly foundered on the rocks of man's perversity. Even today our heavy emphasis on education is rooted in the forlorn hope that young people can be taught to become self-governing adults of independent cast of mind. But the more we teach, ironically, the farther we seem to slip from the ideal of a democratic individualism, and now the notion of salvation through individuality is the property of a few moral aristocrats. It was the noblest of secular visions and its perversion through the mayhem of the kid cults leaves a terrible void, an aching sadness. The stark problem facing western societies is not unleashing more individuality, but trying to keep a community from disintegrating under the heel of licentious individualists.

There is some hope of discovering a salvation through science, or rather through the expansion of knowledge, empirically tested. This is particularly the vision of the behavioral sciences which are pinching and probing the human psyche as never before in a desperate effort to formulate some means of erecting a rational social order. These good social doctors work with amoral tools: not rights or wrongs, but models of personality uninformed by any vision of good and evil, God or devil. And the result is, so far, utterly forlorn. Typically it boils down to some "scientific" recommendation that pornography laws be abandoned because there is no negative impact discernible upon the viewer or reader. The irony of this sad quest is that science has no moral authority. It might be able to prove empirically that morals achieve such and such results within the community, but such empirical finding is scarcely a clarion call to mankind to behave in some way. Science has no trumpets.

The prospect of a mankind that will continue to be perverse, sinful, mean, and ignorant appalls the apostate church—or at least the evolved church that has somehow wed the Christian faith to the secular liberal ethic of reform. For such clergy and congregations, especially the swinging Unitarians, the whole purpose of religion has become liberal reform. The Unitarian tenet frankly holds that mankind is naturally good and perfectible. In a beliefless church, this is tacitly dogma. Such liberals regard the idea of an unredeemable world as repulsive pessimism: education, freedom, the evolution of the state, redistribution of income, etc. are surely the paths to redemption. There is an exquisite irony in Unitarian literature: the clearly defined enemies that absorb Unitarian polemicists are the orthodox and traditional churches, rather than the evils that surround us. The Unitarians ritualistically assail dogma or Catholic authoritarianism, or creed, or orthodoxy, or religious conformity, as evils. Read a piece of proselytizing Unitarian literature and your enemy will be quickly identified not as thieves, murderers, perverts, profaners, etc., but the other denominations, and especially those that insist that God is God, and Jesus is His son. God is a swinger, and Jesus is a cool cat.

That leaves, finally, the vision of salvation held by the Christian remnant, the vision rejected and despised by most secular and liberal men; by every gnostic reformer on earth. It begins with the proposition that man is fallen, i.e., perpetually perverse and wicked because since Adam, there has been no way he can govern his lusts and rages and selfishness. It means, further, that no social reform can do much more than ameliorate immediate distress, and that it will have little ultimate impact on man's perverse nature. But the remnant also undersands that through the cross, individual men can bond themselves to God anew, and achieve forgiveness, love, mercy, charity, and innate goodness. But the Kingdom of Heaven is not something that resides in nations, or peoples, or society, or groups, but rather within private souls. Unlike the secular liberal who treats "society" as a thing, a unity to be pinched, probed, and reformed, the Christian considers society an agglomeration of individuals, including himself. Thus, to the extent he is able to reform himself, he does reform society. Indeed, if a large number of individuals were able to achieve the sublime selfless love of Christianity, the social problems of the secular world would evanesce. It is the Christian insight that each of us is a social problem. We are all fallen. Neither the kids in Woodstock Nation nor the liberals envision themselves as social problems, but rather seek the reform of society, from which they are alienated because society is the alleged repository of all evil. They distort the Christian equation, and assume each individual is naturally good and able to pursue a beautiful life but for the evils of society, which strangle virtue in the crib. This is the central myth of the flower children: we are good innocents; the old world, the beast called society, is evil and trying to clutch us to its corrupt bosom, and we shall resist and even tear evil society asunder so that we may be free in our innocence. If that is a myth, it is a particularly gripping myth, and one that is fostered by the liberal elders who have encouraged the kids. If the kids find society alien, they find the Establishment—the power holders—even more so. It is impossible now, at this eleventh hour, for the young to believe that those who hold great power arrived there innocently or virtuously, or function in that capacity with good intent. They "understand" Mr. Nixon not as a man who dreams of a better Republic, more virtuous and just and good, but a

38

man motivated solely by political calculation, a chameleon who will change colors with the greening of America. The understanding is grotesque. It is worse than cynicism. The same thread runs through their assessment of nearly every man of achievement: there is none on top, in business and government, who didn't lie, cheat, steal, chicane, knife, and bully to arrive where he is, no matter if he is a George Romney, Lyndon Johnson, or (perish the thought) Eugene McCarthy. That such men may have arrived at their positions of eminence because of greater virtue and decency and industry—as did James Cash Penney—is scarcely considered or immediately rejected.

There are nominal Christians who say within themselves: "I am good and the world is evil." Such are in danger of blinding themselves to their own iniquities, especially if they define goodness in a negative way, as avoiding sin, rather than positively, such as going out into the world with all mercy, love, and charity for others. But the intuition that the world is evil is a proper part of Christian belief and is held in common with secular flower children. The difference is that most Christians understand they have a long way to go before arriving at personal goodness, and therefore they are a part of the world's evil, whereas most hip youngsters assume their own goodness, and don't believe they are one of society's "social problems." Beyond that, the kids tend to reject definitions of good and evil, and thus feel the problems besetting the world are void of moral content. The kids have turned this attitude into a fine art, applying no moral criteria to themselves at all, but judging their parents according to their parents' standards.

It is the Christian insight that no man can ever justify himself through good works alone, even if those works have a redemptive value for society and himself. There must be faith. With good works a devout man can do much: with love he can supply grace and courage to his neighbors, give good gifts, and defend the oppressed. A great many devout men can ameliorate enormous distress in the world. But this vision of good works is not utopian. It does not suppose a day will come when there is no longer distress because all are cared for, comforted, and educated. It is reasonable rather than idyllic. The vision of a New Jerusalem is not of this world. The world is intractable because man is fallen. Salvation lies in absolute faith in the Redeemer. This hurdle of faith is where secular men turn away. The more sensitive among them applaud the good works of Christianity, and some find empirical reasons to foster religion as a boon to society. But along the barrier of faith they halt, unwilling to accept the Master or believe in heaven for the redeemed soul. It antagonizes them that Christian doctrine can't reside cheek by jowl with the whole pantheon of values; that Christianity would not reside in ancient times side by side with the pagan gods of Rome, but had to triumph or go underground. So many secular men would like to permit Christianity to flourish as a sort of cult or sect, but not all-powerful and without making its unique claim on its adherents and all of mankind. In the end, secular men must line up against the church and drive it underground because of the intransigent and total allegiance of Christians to Christ, which is an unbearable affront to the cosmopolitan, secular, tolerant world. All our values are now in flux, but the core of Christianity is not in flux. When the pioneer hippies invade the territory of the Church of Christ, they will arrive, in the end, at the narrow door of faith that has illumined the world for two millennia. They will choose either to enter or die.

Some of the young have tried to fashion a personal salvation and even social salvation from the notion of copping out. This is the religion of Timothy Leary and his sycophants. It follows from the belief that "society" but not "self" is unspeakably corrupt and forever in the hands of the evil Establishment. If society is evil, then the one way the alien individual can preserve his innocence and integrity is total withdrawal: negate all the pressures and be free. Even the positive social pressures, such as admonitions to this or that worthy cause are seen by the cop-outs as being cynically motivated to preserve the system, rather than as simple appeals to charity. The cop-outs truly cop out. Mostly they seek to disappear from the awareness of secular authorities and function as invisible men. Whereas the radicals are vengeful destroyers, the cop-outs are the uncommitted hermits, male and female. Most of them scrape some sort of living only to expend it in drugs. Others are succored by the garrisons of mercy that an alarmed society has stationed around such districts as Haight-Ashbury to sustain collapsed and broken bodies. Of all the versions of utopia, the cop-out one is the most pathetic. It involves a flight into total loneliness and resistance to every tug of the heart to join others and stumble onward somehow to a better life. It is a prescription for madness. The drug cop-out lives in a world of total narcissism, egoistic rather than egotistic—gradually loosening the means by which he communes with others. Every trip is a trip alone even when he is surrounded by others. Every psychedelic delusion, or jolt of speed, or surrealistic sensation, is experienced alone and is without meaning, even in a room full of people. Life is reduced to a Dali painting and when the landscapes pall, there is nothing beyond but the asylum. It is the only version of utopia that involves a voluntary retreat into solitary confinement. It is the only version of utopia that fosters the death of self and abandonment of all others. Even the hatred of others—such as motivates the radicals—is more expressive of

40

vitality than the abandonment of the cop-out. The flower children are actually hothouse flowers, so bruised by huff and chuff of daily life that they must retreat to their orchid asylums. Orchids are parasites, and the drop-outs are parasites as well, subsisting on the mercy of those who care. Perhaps that is their ultimate intent, if they have any—forcing the world to care. They die so young, and the death is merciful. A few, such as those in the New Mexico communes, achieve a sort of listless new life. But these are the few, and are the ones with stronger fibre. In the end their innocence and integrity are breached anyway and they are nourished by the Establishment they condemn.

No paradise juts above the horizon: not in drugs, nor science, nor humane liberalism, nor individualism. In orthodox Christianity the sorrows of man are at least ameliorated and the struggle to perfect the self has meaning. But the New Jerusalem awaits the decisions of God and is beyond the architectural capacity of man. All this is not a matter of pessimism, but of joy for a Christian. That a way exists is all that a Christian asks—all any human can ask. And that the struggle day by day, through all the sorrows of the flesh in the world, through disease and despair, poverty and emotional collapse, through frustration and impotence, through boredom and war, through winters and the spring—to survive and grow, all in proper season and according to the grace we receive—all this had meaning of its own, and is cherished as the triumph of life over death. We grow in adversity and are privileged to serve God unto the end of time, playing the trumpets of Christ the Messiah, and waving the banners of the host of the heavens. But only a few will achieve that. For many, the roads to salvation will descend gradually to a blackness and the banks of the inky river where love is gone and hope and glory have fled, and even the echoes never return.

4. REVOLUTIONARY GAMES

THE revolution of the alienated kids is unique in the history of revolutions because it is not serious; it is an elaborate game. The kids are not ragged, starving zealots at the foot of a Bastille or Winter Palace. By and large they are happy, well-fed, laughing grotesques with an enormous amount of freedom and opportunity guaranteed them by a society that treats them kindly indeed. They have the opportunity to pursue a myriad of fruitful careers. Except for the blacks, they do not picket and bomb and organize to protest deep injustice to themselves or their families. They are not poor, nor are their parents. They are not sealed into the borders of the United States, unable to emigrate elsewhere as is the case in the Soviet Union.

Their version of revolution is to outfox authority and embarrass those who maintain order. Unlike the earlier anarchists who bombed to kill, the youngsters allegedly bomb only property, and when a math student at the University of Wisconsin is killed by bombing, most of them regret it. They have no unified manifesto or revolutionary vision: no secular bible with a promise of utopia in it for those who pursue the revolution to its bitter conclusion. They dally with shocking things such as treason, but more for the daringness of it than to form alliances with the enemies of the Republic.

They do serious things, seriously considered, to stop the machine, but these dwindle to frivolity and foolishness. The Yippies are clowns; the drug cultists are inwardly corroded cop-outs unable to sustain a militant revolution; the Weathermen have no real ideology, no vision of some joyous new world to inspire them, and so their efforts are sporadic, petulant, and grounded in century-old Marxist cliches. The great mass of fellow-traveling students and street people around the universities is unorganized, self-centered, and only sporadically inflamed against the "pigs" of repression. Serious revolution requires serious cadres organized into subversive cells, which work under total puritan discipline and with total zeal. It requires master plans and organizing genius and the violent attrition of governors until the revolutionary force is feared and respected by the rulers of the state. All these are lacking, and the government response so far has been even more indolent and haphazard than the young radicals.

If the revolution were in earnest, the government would soon find ways to smash it in earnest. To allege that the government is currently repressive is laughable, considering the options and pressures available to those in power. The kids will never even experience authentic repression—the star chamber, concentration camp, torture—so long as the Republic remains commited to liberal and religious values and eschews totalitarianism. When the enemies of the state are lined up against the wall and shot down like cordwood, without trial, without quarter, then it could be said that the United States government is beginning to suppress revolution, instead of amiably counterpunching the kids' haymakers.

There is a tantalizing question about the kids' motives: if the government and society were to grant young radicals their every demand, and let them reorganize the Republic along their own lines, without resistance, would the youngsters be any less alienated by American society? Or would they be even more contemptuous of it, more alienated than before? The question is valid because it is possible the underlying intent for all the revolutionary ferment is to force their elders to assert some values, some boundaries, some norms, and enforce them in a way that suggests that civil democracy, representative government, personal morals and ethics, and faith in God all have genuine meaning to those who pay them lip service.

That is to say, our crop of revolutionaries may not even believe at bottom in its own propaganda. Unquestionably there is rot and corruption in America: a cynical capitalism that exploits ruthlessly, hand in glove with an honorable capitalism inspired by high ethical ideals. There are callousness and racism as charged. There is an affluent class that expends its treasure on foolishness and material things rather than the spiritual needs and hungers, as charged. There is a bloated oppressive bureaucracy as a result of decades of liberalistic tinkering, and it is a leech on the blood

44

of productive citizens—as charged. There are plenty of things wrong, but one of them is not that government is unresponsive to needs. Congress and the bureaus and state agencies have tripped over themselves in recent decades to set up poverty programs, pollution programs, health care programs, etc. A President has unraveled the war as fast as diplomacy and power politics dictate. The unresponsiveness—if it exists—lies in the impotence of liberal programs rather than in the system, which if anything is too responsive to resist mass pressure. Liberalism has, probably, created far more poverty than it has affluence. High taxes, rising minimum wages, closed shop unionism, and a host of other programs have radically reduced the number of jobs and the ease of entering the job market, as well as consumer spending, and new business. The resultant growth of welfare and still more poverty programs adds even more unproductive bureaucracy to the burden already carried by productive persons and business.

The kids are engaged in revolution for its own sake. The object is not utopia or reform, nor a benevolent concern for others. They are alienated first and then work back to the various issues to feed their alienation. They fasten upon issues such as the draft, which they view in wholly personal terms, as a repressive state measure that ought to be evaded. Issues are mere vehicles for their game; conflicts to be exploited. The victory of the cadres is not followed by a cessation of revolutionary activism but rather a sudden appetite for some objective that had hitherto been out of reach. In fact, the acquiescence of authorities is usually seen as further proof that America is rotten and that it no longer has values.

In a sense, the young are probing to find out how much value, how much belief, still resides in America, and the more they are permitted to rampage the deeper is their feeling that American society is corrupt, valueless, cynical, and selfish. The social issues are scarcely even a point of serious contention, but are rather revolutionary tools to motivate fair-minded nonrevolutionary students into a sporadic mass violence. The issues such as racism, real or imagined, are handy myths to exploit and build. The myths of the military-industrial complex, the wealthy Republicans, the lack of freedom in America, etc., have grains of truth, but the point is that they are believable to the young and become the devil theories of the revolution. Every revolution, including that of the kids, must have its devils and it doesn't matter whether the devils are fabricated as long as they are believed to be real.

Ironically, the kids and their constant needling of values are demonstrating in a circular way that there is some fundamental truth in their charge that America is corrupt. They probably are not consciously aware that they are probing deep through the layers of decaying belief and that

45

when they finally encounter true resistance they are also encountering that which is yet valid and noble to most Americans. Perhaps the young radicals are performing a service for us all by revealing the depths of nihilism and cynicism in America. What the kids are discovering is that their elders don't give a damn about much of anything, and least of all about moral and spiritual convictions. The kids may half-consciously be less interested in overthrowing the whole society than in stripping away the phony, flabby residual values left over from an earlier age, to leave only the hard, firm core of American belief. In this sense, the bulk of their contempt must be directed toward their liberal mentors who have led the demolition squads. If the professors believe in little or nothing moral and spiritual, then the professors and their campus colleagues should be the first to acquiesce in the kids' demands—and that in fact has been the case on campus after campus.

An authentic revolutionary is usually radicalized by personal and social calamity, such as personal ugliness, weakness, lack of character, inferior or superior intelligence, perverse parents, deep privation and misery, or the collapse of verities. Or, if he is sensitive he may be revolutionized by deep social injustice for some class, widespread poverty, lack of freedom, excessive taxation, repressive government, or other social cancers.

The revolutionary kids rarely are alienated by these conditions out of their past, but rather by what they consider to be an unbearable future. Most have never starved, never lacked amenities nor schooling nor freedom nor state justice. Most have been so personally bitter with self-hatred that they blame all of society for their private troubles. They are, perhaps, a weak and overprotected generation. Their parents deemphasized strong character and emphasized personality and adjustment, and this hurt them.

They have never known the terror of the Gestapo knock at 3:00 a.m.; nor the fright of a Cossack raid on their town; nor the sudden disappearance of friends and family into the hands of the MVD. They have never experienced the rattle of machine guns firing into civilian populations, nor state decrees nailed on the doors of businesses and shops, forbidding further commerce; nor star chambers and torture cells; nor arrests for writing or speaking any defiant thing. The ingenious weapons of the twentieth-century total state are deployed all over the world, but rarely in America; yet it is America they loathe and compare with Nazism. This suggests some disjunction between reality and belief. There is simply no ground to accuse the Republic of totalitarianism, especially in a period of incredible leniency. Moreover, the gates of the Republic are not closed:

46

immigration is possible. Unlike the Soviet Union, the United States permits the disaffected to leave in peace. The Port of New York is not barbed wire, mine fields, machine guns, and helmeted troops.

Much of the revolutionary literature reads as though it were a great put-on. Jerry Rubin's book, *Do It*, is more campy porno than a manifesto. None of the literature expresses any deep, moving outrage at American society—at least not with the power and gravity of the Old Left's writings. But rather, it concentrates on the arts of revolution, the method rather than substance. The essence of the New Left literature is technique: how to bomb, how to shock, how to organize. This suggests two possibilities: either the intended readers already take for granted the need to overthrow the régime, or else the unconscious intent of these revolutionary manuals is a kind of permissive game; a demolition of the flabby values Americans profess only in the breech, but not a demolition of America. True revolutionary literature is moving, soul searching, searing. It is angry and passionate. It builds a case. The manifestoes of the New Left are all camp and poppycock. They do not move, nor are they passionate.

Today's youth radicalism is chic and camp. It is a game, a life-style in its own right, played against irate government with real stakes and real penalties, such as fines and imprisonment. But a game nonetheless. It is an anti-authority game, with one side challenging every remaining value in civilization and the other side forced to defend values it finds genuine, and surrender the ones not worth defending any more. The tender, passionate, powerful writings of authentic revolution are absent from the underground press, which is more inclined to shock squares than to build a following of convinced, alienated comrades, motivated by a rage against the system. There is no puissance in the *East Village Other*; no tenderness in the *Los Angeles Free Press*; no lengthy dialectics on communal life and anticapitalist philosophy in all the shabby little underground sheets across the Republic. The youth radicalism has all the earmarks of a corrupt liberalism rather than a reinvigorated and ruthless communism, and perhaps that is why there has been a persistent gulf between the Old and New Left. The kids have, by and large, reduced the older liberal values to license and mayhem.

There is something quite lovely about the flower children who are not so radical. Theirs is a different revolution, without the intensity of the Weathermen or the lunacy of the pharmaceutical utopians. They are nature's children and when they slip a daisy into the barrel of a National Guardsman's rifle, they are performing a certain moral act that speaks well for the future of man: it is an affirmation of life over death, living matter over cold steel. It is also, alas, a rejection of values. Perhaps there is something in it of the older mysticism: there were charismatic Indians who had great visions and thought themselves immune to the paleface bullets, but the realities of physics predominated in the end. The insertion of a flower into a rifle muzzle is a way of saying "see, you need not fear us; we are harmless and we shall disarm you with love. The flower prevents you from shooting your wintery bullets into the springtime of youth." But there are darker aspects: the daisy becomes a delicate defiance of authority. Perhaps that should be, if the authority is unjust or built on corrupt values. Perhaps an overly fearful society ought not to interpose the National Guard whenever the flower children stroll. On the other hand, the calling of the guard may be based on the intuition that the flower children are immature and full of barely repressed mayhem, and therefore are as likely to erupt into crazy and damaging tumults as to wander peacefully, a bearded, beaded, bra-less bunch, through the town squares. It is hard to know about flower children: they are as likely to include Manson family types as they are the little intellectual nymphs studying antiquities at the museum. They are, precisely, children. Their intellects are self-centered; their vision of love and peace is simple and childish, and their daisies suggest they are not ready to put away childish things.

There is no reason to believe the flower children are deeply alienated from existing society. They function rather well in it. There is no impulse to immigrate elsewhere. Unlike some of the Amish, who have been quietly moving to Latin America because they believe the Republic no longer offers them the freedom to practice their quiet, tranquil faith and life style, the flower children are not potential émigrés. Their pleasure in being mildly radical in a tolerant society betrays them. Their ideas are not discernibly different from orthodox liberalism except that they are visceral rather than intellectually organized. Strip a beflowered hippie and you'll usually discover a naked liberal. The alienation is all that is different. Hippies literally wear the clothes of revolt; the hair of ostracism they wish upon themselves. The shaggy beards and the long locks of the ladies are worn expressly to offend the straight people. It is part of the game, the fad, the chic revolution. An authentic revolutionary dresses in a manner to avoid all attention; his goal is to be inconspicuous rather than offensive. Hippiedom is an attitude: a cultural, stylistic revolt rather than an intellectual posture with the overthrow of the Establishment as its goal.

They call themselves freaks, a word defined as (1) a sudden and apparently causeless change or turn of events, the mind, etc.; an apparently capricious notion, occurrence; (2) any abnormal product or curiously un-

48

usual object, an aberration; (3) a person or animal on exhibition as an example of some strange deviation from nature, monster. (*Random House Dictionary*)

Their choice of words is not accidental. A freak is some strange deviation from nature; a monster on display for all to see. A freak is an apparently causeless or capricious turn of events or occurrence. Causeless and capricious, perhaps the most important factors of being alienated. The thing to bear in mind is that the underlying compulsion to become a freak may have little to do with the professed grievances they express toward straight society. There is no reason to suppose the freaks are less blind to their own quirks than the rest of us. Their apt selection of the word *freak* suggests some conscious assessment of their worth.

Nothing in the word *freak* suggests an alienation based on valid grounds: suffering or indignities or repression, but rather the word suggests a departure from nature, or from a natural order that governs things. The very word suggests that there is a normalcy in the universe. Without norms, or order, or orthodoxy, there could not be freaks. Nothing could be bizarre if everything is bizarre.

The kids also use the word to mean "mania." They talk of drug freaks, or hair freaks, and what they mean is drug or hair maniacs; ones with an obsessive and compulsive need, or fascination with drugs or hair, or whatever. Maniacs are essentially slaves; persons trapped by an obsessive lust. Thus, the very definition the kids apply to themselves ranges from monsters to slaves, or in any case persons who arrived at their status without apparent reason, capriciously.

But the reasons are probably there, and probably run back several centuries, if not back to the Fall of Man. They have little to do with ecology. Or racism. Or the evils of the Establishment. Or the evolution of mass populations. Or capitalism. Or the seniority system in Congress. Or the deaths of John and Robert Kennedy and Martin Luther King. Or the atom bomb. For generations, the brilliant, questing, secular, skeptical genius of the West has broadened the frontiers of knowledge, especially knowledge of the natural universe. The process has gradually revealed the laws of nature; man has learned that matter is governed by immutable, mathematically precise allocations of energy. The advancement of science has been built on the discovery of natural law, and the adoption of physics to our use. The same skeptical spirit has been applied to man: we know infinitely more about man's body and brain and social transactions but not enough about the laws governing our relations to each other. These are still a matter of faith. Secular men persist in a curious argument: they admit to

49

a natural law governing physical matter. They admit, that is, to the validity of physics as an explanation of the functioning of the universe. They admit to such constants as gravity and to the theory that $E=MC^2$. But they don't admit that man is governed by similar norms. The religious man discovers these laws through faith; secular men have attempted to find some norms through the social sciences but have simply sunk into a morass of speculation about man's nature, with the tacit conclusion that if such norms exist they are undiscoverable.

The secular young freaks, the products of the secular society, can discover no such norms, but obviously intuit that norms should exist, or they wouldn't label themselves freaks. To the extent they believe in norms they believe in George Gallup as a substitute for God. Norms are what the majority are. But that fallacy is obvious to most everyone except social scientists. The only authority secular men accept is that of science, and to date science has been unable to demonstrate norms, or laws of human conduct, that would inevitably, ineffably lead to—what? an earthly utopia? personal joy? All else in the universe is governed by physics and biological imperatives. The survival of the species. But intelligent man, while subject to the laws of physics and the imperatives of biology, also thinks and has a dynamic will, and the freedom to choose between objectives. The religious man believes that such norms are undiscoverable except through faith, and that if science should approximate universal norms of conduct and determine valid goals those norms should achieve, they still lack authority. Human nature is perverse enough to defy authority, and man's perversity will surely defy mere scientific formulations. Surely there are few secular liberals, even now, willing to concede an immutable code of norms or laws that ought to govern human conduct. There is not even agreement on what such laws ought to achieve, much less what the norms ought to be. That leaves, in essence, only revealed Christianity as the source of social authority. And it leaves a body of secular freaks, defying God for no reason they can comprehend.

The youth revolution is only superficially an icon-smashing trip. The sacred things, the stable things, the transcendent things were already desanctified by secular liberals before the youth cults evolved. The hierarchies of value were demolished by muckrakers and skeptics: they thought they had dethroned God. The kids are essentially acting out what the liberals only dared fantasize: free sex, free dress codes; freedom from the puritan work ethic. Abandonment of tradition. But beyond this is a restless search among them, or at least the ones not depraved, for the very thing they scorn; indeed for the authority they profess to hate but which they intuit will guide them out of hopelessness; and beyond that, for God. Their revolution is unique because it is only outwardly revolutionary; within, it is a desperate, calamitous, circular search for some God, some master, some authority before which to kneel and discover one's own soul and worth.

An authentic revolution does not proceed suicidally, and it provokes authority as little as possible until the time of the coup. It fosters discontents, not hostility. Most authentic revolutionaries are puritanical because licentiousness dissipates revolutionary energy and intensity. However twisted and labyrinthine the true revolutionary soul, it does not usually manifest itself in narcissistic display designed to antagonize the orthodox. A revolutionary is a man obsessed with the belief that a new political organization will usher in a better world, and a happier life for himself.

Essential to any revolutionary situation is a deep gulf between the prevailing social beliefs and practices on the one hand, and the beliefs of the revolutionaries on the other. On this basis, the youth cults are scarcely radical at all, while the most radical groups in America are the libertarian conservatives. The left-wing youth cults deviate scarcely at all—except perhaps in drug use—from establishment liberalism. The kids believe in the efficacy of science; in regulating or abolishing private business; in moderate socialism; in moral latitude; in the idea that persons are victims of their environment. They do not accept totalitarian communism by and large, but they flirt with aspects of it. They believe in the welfare state, social security, medicare, food stamps, nationalized welfare benefits, an income floor, poverty programs, government job training, free education through college, etc. They believe in personal and sexual freedom in areas tabooed by religion, and in a state that doesn't invade private moral options. They believe in the traditional liberal open society with free ingress and egress and complete freedom of expression. On the other hand, they believe in rigorous economic planning, state management of business, progressive taxation, and a large public sector.

All this is scarcely revolutionary or even radical. It is liberal orthodoxy clothed in hippie beads. It is establishmentarianism with a touch of violence, beards, and beads. It is secularism with a bit of witchcraft and wackiness. Now consider the estranged young conservative libertarian and how genuinely radical are his views vis-à-vis today's establishment orthodoxies. He believes in reducing the federal government to perhaps half its existing size and generally limiting its activity to defense and securing domestic tranquility. He is for abolishing most welfare, social security, and poverty programs. He would repeal most labor legislation and union-monopoly protections. He opposes most regulation of business, consumer

51

protection legislation, and regulatory agencies and would substitute a free market in their stead. He believes in federalism with virtually sovereign state governments. He rejects minimum wage laws and most other work and labor regulation. He rejects tariffs and quotas and other devices to protect business and labor. He prefers a gold standard with floating international exchange rates. He would cut federal taxes to the point of being a minor burden on individuals. He is an advocate of laissez-faire, and of the moral and ethical underpinnings that make a free economy, with its blossoming opportunity, feasible.

All these things are anathema—literally horrors—to the bulk of Americans from the center leftward, and even to most people on the moderate right. The true radicals—but not revolutionaries—in the United States today are the libertarians who wish to unleash capitalism rather than throttle it. There is nothing on the left, or in the kid cult ideologies, that equals the radical position of the conservative libertarians; nothing that creates a gap so vast between the center and the extreme. Perhaps that is why the Establishment is so silent about the young rightists, who don't receive even 1 percent of the publicity accorded the young radical leftists. It is a reasonable supposition that the Establishment hates and fears the "radical right" but is much more comfortable with the radical left. If the right-wing youngsters are correct, then almost everything the liberal Establishment believes in will prove wrong; but if the programs of the radical left prove right, then the views of the Establishment will in the main be justified. The revolutionary kids are comfortingly close to orthodox centrist liberalism. The young rightist is teleologically far out, in fact beyond the pale. If the revolutionary kids do manage to overthrow the *ancien régime*, their prescriptions won't be unfamiliar. There isn't a radical bone in Tom Hayden's head, nor has anything radical emerged from Norman Mailer's belly. And Timothy O'Leary, guru of the drug cult, prescribes placebos.

All this is to suggest that there is not an adequate gulf between the moderate liberal Establishment and the kid cults to warrant a revolutionary situation. That suggests another basic reason why the young revolution is a game, a charade, rather than a concerted effort to topple society. Only the blacks, primarily through the Panthers, are instigating anything like a revolution: and they appear to be less interested in demolishing the white world than in establishing enclaves in it, or seceding from it; black Vaticans in white Italys.

Half a century ago, a yawning, unbridgeable chasm existed between individualist, Christian, capitalist America, and the handful of revolutionary communists and anarchists who sought to overthrow society and install a collectivist one. The radicals of that period were as alienated from the established mainstream as the young libertarians on the right are today—indeed, even more so. But in the intervening decades the gap has closed precipitously so that the *zeitgeist* has nearly merged with the young revolutionary activists. Indeed, there is a certain absurdity in the fact that the liberals like to consider themselves alienated and slightly radical vis-à-vis the rest of America, and the older pre-New Deal orthodoxies. And some Establishment types even feel alienated from their direct political forebears, the New Deal liberals. In turn, the New Left feels alienated and revolutionary vis-à-vis the liberal Establishment, although the helmsmen of the New Left have set their compass only a few degrees to the left of the Establishment. The bonding of revolutionary and governor results in a new politics of change, an obsession with change as the major goal of politics regardless of the beneficial or damaging result of that change. Much of the change may simply be a slowing of revolutionary capitalism but whether that is good or bad is less important to the left than whether it is a certified "reform" that further expands the public sector.

It is a commonplace cliche that we live in a period of accelerating change. The change is obvious in the flood of processes, comforts, new sports, new transportation, new technology, etc., that we see constantly. It is equally commonplace to say change is pouring over us so rapidly that our institutions and citizens can't cope with it. It is less frequently asserted that the bulk of change is the fruit of revolutionary capitalism financing basic research and converting new knowledge into commercial gain. There is a progress permeating the business, scientific, and technical worlds that supplies an illusion of change to the less changeable things around the penumbra, such as morals, human nature, ideals of justice and virtue, etc. So much is change the orthodoxy of every discipline and politics that the man who asserts the world, or at least morals and human nature, isn't changing is apt to be considered daft or blind. Change is the orthodoxy and those who discern rapid change are more orthodox than the gradualists and foot-draggers. Revolution, that is, forms the reality of our politics. At bottom the Establishment considers itself just as revolutionary as the kid cults. The New Deal was a revolution; so was the Fair Deal of Harry Truman, and after the Eisenhower interregnum the New Frontier revolutionaries ushered in Camelot, followed by the Great Society revolution.

The irony of these latter revolutions is that they are anything but radical. They promote change, or the promise of change, without actually varying the thrust of "progress." There was a time when change was regarded with suspicion, as the enemy of tranquil social orders and as a downhill rather than uphill phenomenon. Change was the harbinger of worsening circumstance. Today the reverse is true and change, any change, is considered optimistically as the promise of better days. That optimism prevails even in a century that produced an Adolph Hitler and Joseph Stalin. But even as the New Left adopts more and more trappings of change, such as revolutionary talk, consciously adapts new modes of grooming and manners, the radical content seems to evaporate. When revolution is the orthodoxy of both Establishment and those allegedly alienated, the only true radical is the naysayer who yells "stop" at the crossroads of history. If flux is the orthodoxy, then the true alienated radical is the one who insists that some things—such as God or God's law—don't ever change and cannot be reinterpreted or made "relevant" (i.e., more flexible to conform to the universal flux of all institutions). In these circumstances, the libertarian conservative is doubly radical, for not only does he insist that there are unchanging religious values and ethical ideals, but he is also willing to ride the unleashed tiger of laissez-faire capitalism. The alienated kids are neither alienated nor radical and it is rare that they advance an idea that is shocking to anyone except a few maiden aunties. No matter what they try—witchcraft, drugs, yogi, nudity, communal living, obscenity, mayhem, or bombing public buildings—cosmopolitan sophisticates absorb the minishock waves easily. People take it all in stride. New York and San Francisco are unflappable.

If your potty little revolution is plotted along the exact trajectory plotted by your country's progressives, then your revolution is more fun and frolic than drastic change. And if no great gulf separates you from your straight, square peers who are also more or less revolutionary, then what you are doing is sanitary, antiseptic, and quite safe. If you are a leftist and the revolutionary clouds on the horizon are your clouds instead of their clouds—then you can look forward to progress and fun.

The one unbearable thought for any leftist is a revolution in a different direction such as the triumph of the economic libertarians. Or the triumph of a new church affirming faith in God's law and the capacity of religious, self-governing men to do without the huge service state erected by the left. Or an antiegalitarian revolution that evolved hereditary aristocracy. Or, simply, a revolution that virtually abolished the state and transferred social services to capitalist corporations. These are all radical departures, hence alarming to the ideologues whose vision of progress is statist and egalitarian.

The goal of the revolutionary kids is not to foment a revolution but to be a revolutionary. Revolutions are not chic, but being a revolutionary is. And they are achieving their goal easily—with dire effects on the rest of society which tends more and more toward repressive action. They talk of

54

sacrifice and danger and enemies and romantic conspiracy and indeed they experience all these things abundantly. It will be something to tell their grandchildren, early next century. The only trouble is, if they succeed in turning a major segment of the public into revolutionaries, they might end up with a revolution. But not their revolution. The other kind. The kind that Lenin and Trotsky spurred and organized relentlessly.

5. POLITICS

WHEN it comes to partisan politics, the kids are a new breed. Not only are they independents in the traditional sense but also they reject the established parties altogether, along with the partisan politics that fuels their existence. A great many supported "Clean Gene" McCarthy, the Minnesota Democrat, in 1968; but the kids were not formally Democrats, and, indeed, much of their antagonism was vented directly at the traditional Democratic Party. The enemy was not so much Hubert Humphrey nor Mayor Daley as the structure—the venerable edifice that is rooted in wards and in patronage and topped by the national committee. The kids supposed the structure was corrupt and unresponsive and under the vassalage of powerful barons who controlled votes often without regard for plebiscitary feelings. Hubert Humphrey—for decades as much or more a liberal than Eugene McCarthy—was cast as the enemy because he stuck to the machine and McCarthy was the outrider. It did not matter that Humphrey's overall record was more innovative and left-seeking than McCarthy's; Humphrey had, in his latter days, supported the Vietnam war, faithfully echoing Lyndon Johnson—and that, ipso facto, wiped out decades of liberalism and made him an Establishment whore. The kids, however, wanted a latter-day saint.

The kid cults showed little interest in the Republicans and their convention. The GOP was less kid-cultish than the Democrats; indeed, beyond redemption and, therefore, not worth harrying, except in a perfunctory way to embarrass Richard Nixon. The difference was this: the kids scarcely tried to alter the vector of the GOP and its leaders. They worked from outside, worked as enemies of the whole party, and sought to embarrass the party regardless of who the Republican candidate would be.

But the kids, even though not formally allied to the Democrats, did try to alter the trajectory of that party from inside, mainly through the McCarthy movement but also through the application of mobocratic disorders through Chicago: marches, confrontations, mayhem, picketing, and, above all, a great gathering of young activists to people the parks and streets and offer a youthful presence that every Democrat would scarcely be able to avoid during his Chicago sojourn.

To the extent the kids have any preference, it is leftward, and therefore Democratic. (The exception is the conservative youth group, Young Americans for Freedom, which is rightist and was Reagan-oriented.) However, the kids maintain a deeply cynical attitude toward all organized American politics. The pronouncements of the major officeholders are always deemed half-truths and self-serving. Unlike the liberals who still believe politics is a progressive force, the kids are restive and a bit schizophrenic about what they expect from the political process. In one sense they are still True Believers; capture a party, infuse it with their ideology, usher in reforms, elect a leftist national administration—do all this and there will be Progress and a more humane world, more just and equal and peaceful; people will be happy and more comfortable; poverty, war, and racism will vanish. This is the vision of liberalism and many kids accept it. At the same time, they reject it. Partisan politics produces only a deadlock of action and reaction; the programs are always corrupted if not by Congress, then the bureaucracy, or gutted by Republican administrations, or cause unanticipated messes, or are taken over by the hateful military-industrial complex. This is the cynicism that fostered the slogan, "Power to the People," and it is based on the recognition that all leftist programs from the New Deal onward have gone awry, or have cracked up somehow, or become altogether absurd in current contexts. This cynical analysis, however, never questions the basic rightness or purity of the secular leftist vision. Rather, it assumes that men are going to corrupt the program along the way from the original social idea to the implementation of it by government. Thus, in a sense, even those who reject American politics per se still are believers in the ultimate efficacy of political-collectivist "solutions." The notion that the state can make things better for all is the sine qua non of leftist ideology, and the possibility that some sort of statist reform is not the road to utopia or at least comfortable existence, is the unbearable alternative. "Power to the People," then, does not presuppose an abandonment of public policymaking as the engine of salvation. Rather, it presumes American politics is corrupt and boss-ridden and thwarting the will of the people to have peace, economic leveling, and the end of privilege. There is a certain lovely innocence in the notion, but at bottom it indicts an enormous body of Americans for being not the "people" but the corrupters. That the "people" and the "machine" are virtually the same and deeply intertwined is not generally an admissible observation of the left.

Part of the thrust away from orthodox politics is toward the creation of a New Politics that is more frankly collectivist and radical. Ironically, the New Politics was born not in the crash pads of Haight-Asbury or in Watts, but in the sedate Spanish chambers of the Center for Democratic Institutions at Santa Barbara—the think tank of the Liberal Establishment presided over by Robert Hutchins and his band of frustrated Founding Fathers. There has been, however, a considerable acceptance of the liberal New Politics by the New Left, if only because both share the basic premises. Liberals in the Center are frenetically radicalizing liberal politics to overcome the corruption and inertia of the "machines" governing both major parties. The New Politics envisions urban communes, decentralized government on a local collective basis; more use of militance, picketing, and confrontation; wholesale assaults on established values which drag down reform; and a forthright circumvention of orthodox parties and politics. The New Politics is suitably vague and deliciously radical, and altogether titillating to the graying liberals. Its manifestoes declare that revolution and change are the goals of the New Politics but are quite vague about the direction of revolution or the substance of change. Perhaps literally, any change or any revolution or any erosion of existing institutions is the true goal; in other words, the goal is disorder and flux. The Founding Fathers in Santa Barbara seem bent on revolution for its own sake: salvation is revolution, and the form and content of the revolution are less important than that there be one.

A leftist is usually obsessed with collectivist solutions and the politics of progress. Unlike a square, who can work out his entire life without reference to politics, the leftist perforce becomes a part of a movement, a social enterprise. The square is a private man: his goal may well be to advance himself in business or up the corporate ladder: to provide for his family; to contribute to his church and community. He wishes to go to his grave as a good, contributory citizen. If he has involved himself in politics, the politics have been incidental and usually inclined toward checking statist incursions. But on the left, such a life style is unsatisfactory. Fulfillment consists of agitation for a socialized state, if not nationally then at least through local communes. Liberals are excellent politicians and legislators because their entire outlook is wrapped in the legislative process. The square sees most prospective legislation as a menace to his liberty; the liberal sees it as the advancement of his own idealism.

Builders of abstract political theories have constructed models of a nation with a liberal politics functioning against a conservative politics. The models, while elaborate, are too much the works of cloistered liberal professors who have never understood that conservatism has no politics comparable to that on the left. There was, to be sure, the Goldwater phenomenon, but that was erected—in political terms—on a series of negatives; i.e., of reducing the scope and power of politics on American lives. The politics of the right consist in large measure of reducing the impact of all politics on all citizens. The left, for all its infighting and disunity, is informed by a reformist ideal generally involving expansions of government and deeper political involvement. This overriding ideology generates the ultimate compromises that make liberalism and postliberalism (the secular politics) viable. The liberals literally banish ideology to the right of, say, Richard Nixon, or before him, Dwight Eisenhower, and conclude that anything rightward of that is the paranoia of the crazies and outside the pale. Their spectrum of acceptable politics, that is, moves from the radical left through the various species of progressives and New Leftists, to liberals in the center, and to a narrow band of resisting citizens on the right. They perceive of the band on the right as very narrow, and ascribe a liberal tradition to American politics. A few, such as Ben Wattenburg and Richard Scammon, perceive a larger body of more conservative attitudes that often are not politicized. That is, a large body, perhaps a majority of citizens, have no politics per se, but do have conservative attitudes in various degrees. These attitudes are only occasionally triggered into politics. Mostly, however, private citizens ignore the Potomac hurly burly and simply go about their business, basically accepting what is. They are not active proponents of the system in the sense that, say, William F. Buckley is. Nor do they have a conservative politics in the sense that the unusual New York State Conservative Party has. By and large the sophisticated political models of the Republic ignore them because they are not a political people. Liberals are thus aware of a massive politics on the left, but only a minimal politics on the right, and find themselves at a loss to explain why the "system" resists leftward pressures as much as it does. They conclude erroneously that the "system" does not represent the true leftist-progressive sentiments of most citizens, and is, therefore, corrupt and in the thralldom of bosses and plutocrats and financial barons. It is not. The system is a fairly exact expression of public sentiment. That is, the status quo expresses not only the organized politics of the left and center but also the attitudes unorganized on the center and right. In this respect the existing system is truly democratic, truly representative of the majority public view. It would be less democratic if it were to move leftward, excluding the inarticulate right, the squares whose whole lives have little relationship to what is happening on Pennsylvania Avenue. Here the left is confronted with a dilemma: "Power to the people" already exists in a system that, by and large, represents current attitudes; a system that, by and large, is an accurate reflection of the amalgam of ideas and attitudes of most Americans. While there are, and always will be, pockets of corruption scattered through the structure, it is merely ideology to assert the system itself is corrupt and unresponsive. In fact, the system is astonishingly responsive; perhaps too much so, because the governors of America can scarcely formulate policy on its own merits, without modifying it to appease powerful lobbies and their minions. The notion that the system is unresponsive and politics is in the hands of bosses is a devil-theory to explain away the nonpolitical, unorganized squares whose attitudes influence politics even in these declining days of the Republic. The New Left, of course, does not argue that the system is unresponsive only to themselves; it argues the system is unresponsive to everyone, period. The argument contains a certain irony. For if there is truth in the idea that the system rolls onward, along its own vector, impersonally and ungovernably, it is because decades of leftist programs have vested so much authority and capricious power in the federal bureaus. Political (as opposed to visceral) conservatives have warned against this centralization, this nationalization of power for decades; have warned, precisely, that the responsiveness of all government would diminish in proportion to centralization; that in particular, local and state governments would become the adjuncts of distant bureaus rather than the creatures of the people. And yet, the left, and New Left, complaining about the unresponsiveness of the system, rarely admit their role in building an unresponsive bureaucratic structure, or in weakening responsive local and state institutions.

The New Left cure for the obdurate system is intriguing. By resorting to militance, they plan to bend the system leftward, i.e., away from the established feelings of the mass of Americans. Militance is simply a change in the rules of the game. It is escalation of the conflict: where there were once restraints on political behavior—what were once called civil attitudes—these restraints have been discarded on one side of the fence. Thus, the militants deem it acceptable to portray Richard Nixon as a

61

criminal and murderer, on campus posters—a clear escalation of militance —but it is not okay for the President (or the Vice President) to respond in kind. He is, according to unwritten rules, expected to say only the usual, statesmanlike things; no bare knuckles; no calling the militants any names, even such mild epithets as "effete snobs." A premise of New Left militance, that is, is that it must be used exclusively by the New Left. For any one else to be militant isn't cricket. For Spiro Agnew to return in kind what is dished out is somehow horrendous.

Militance per se does not so much bend the system as destroy it. The unwritten codes of temperance form the rules of warfare between antagonistic social elements: in Congress, men of radically divergent views adhere to a courtesy designed to keep things working, smooth over ruffled feathers, and repair feelings sufficiently to permit future alliances. Much the same temperance exists nationally. Republicans don't, by and large, say and believe all Democrats are pirates, crooks, brigands, lunatics, and idiots. Nor do Democrats really assail the Republicans as wicked, selfish, greedy plutocrats. The point is, words can sting and maul and bite and inflame and, therefore, it is necessary to temper the total pejorative content directed toward political opposition.

As a purely political force, militance has some surprising consequences; for one, it focuses attention on the militants more than on the alleged grievance. For another, the liberals—who cannot conceive of militance without the existence of grave social troubles—rush in with reforms aimed at whatever casual grievance the militants are trumpeting. For another, it leads to laws that deepen the oppressive potential of the state, i.e., to the diminution of the open society. For another, it diverts national energies and resources away from defense and welfare into such nonproductive realms as the expansion of the FBI and Justice Department. For another, to the extent it succeeds, militance breeds more militance until the nation is sporadically ruptured and twisted by disorders, and the political dialogue shifts from a positive emphasis on reform to a negative emphasis on protection. The real impact of militance on politics has been to divert the polemics into a whole new realm. The President is sounding the clarion for internal order; the liberals are exploiting the threat of violence to promote their programs. Congress no longer has the luxury to dawdle lovingly over the placement of new post offices or divvying up the pie offered by the Corps of Engineers or debating whether to add widgets and gismos to the arsenal. Militance has wrought a deterioration in the quality and optimism of politics. Perhaps there are certain beneficial side effects in that too much hope and faith have been traditionally invested in political solutions for problems that rise out of personal weakness. Militance wiped out that unrealistic optimism. No one really believes any more that urban renewal—a nice, cheerful, clean apartment for ex-slum dwellers—will turn a slum roughneck into an upright citizen. But this idea once had common currency on the left, and was once a key rationale offered by liberal urban renewal advocates. At least, Congress has become somewhat more realistic about its own reforming prowess. In a sense, Congress has abandoned liberal optimism. There are liberals populating Congress who ushered in not one or two, but dozens of reforms designed to remedy disorder, eliminate poverty, and guarantee a chicken in every pot; or rather, keep pot from every chick. All this benevolence has not had its intended effect, and only the most dogmatic and obsessed liberals still insist that more government can cure anything. A few liberals doggedly argue that more programs heaped on the existing ones will do the job. But the more open-minded ones are quietly scorning the dogmatists such as Mayor John Lindsay, and in that scorn lies the demise of several centuries of a noble liberal tradition.

It is important, in assessing the politics of the left, to consider the tabooed areas, the programs of the right that are innately antagonistic to liberal-leftist belief, or radical belief, and thus beyond the pale. The very existence of such proposals before Congress rebukes the theory that the left is activist-progressive and the right is passive-reactionary. Such programs are progress to myriads of nonleftist people, and often involve notable advances of private liberty and opportunity and the diminution of excessive state power. But they are taboo because they do not lead to the secular-collectivist utopia that remains the North Star of leftist politics. In general, any movement toward a voluntary structure in social welfare or toward greater entrepreneurial freedom for business, or for lower taxes, and a low-profile government, is considered anathema.

It may be, as in the case of the Interstate Commerce Commission (ICC), that a large body of expert economists believes the transportation industry is overregulated and that the rigidities of regulation keep it—especially the railroads—from achieving economic health. It may be that even President Kennedy, in a rare pragmatic moment, proposed to strip the ICC of much of its power over railroads. It may be that advancing technology has provided competing modes of transportation—buses, planes, trains, trucks, cars, barges—so that King Railroad is dethroned from his monopolistic seat of power. All these things may be true, and yet it is virtually impossible even to get a decent hearing for the question of deregulating the railroads, no matter how demonstrably complex—and mad—the existing rate system is. The reason is that the God of Progress on the left has ordained a continued aggrandizement of power by regulatory agencies.

Thus, not even the creation of a true, competing marketplace in transportation can breach the ideology of century-old liberalism. Ideology is not to be checked by new realities nor by any fact.

Or take social security. So sacred is this cow that its opponents could demonstrate the practicality and superiority of any of several alternatives and be rejected out of hand—indeed, be unable to get a hearing in Congress or in liberal circles. A voluntary, privately funded social security system is beyond the pale—something not even discussed. The doors of the left slam shut so fast and hard on the issue that the possibility of progress toward an uncoerced and more abundant system is nil. There are things wrong with social security: a man contributes for a lifetime but his contributions aren't vested. They cease at death and are not inheritable by the survivors. Moreover, the same premiums invested in private pension funds would double the benefits provided by social security, according to one study. Moreover, the social need to have people provide for their old age could be handled the way automobile liability insurance is: by simply requiring people to establish a pension program that meets minimum standards. Beyond that, people could tailor it to fit their personal needs. All these objections and alternatives are scarcely even discussed or considered on the left because they stem from a rightist provenance, and because the reforms would increase personal options, decrease the governmental role, and therefore diminish the collectivist service state.

There are similar substantial objections to the minimum wage, which destroys jobs, causes high unemployment among marginal workers, and adds to the staggering welfare burden—but because government regulation is *good* per se and a free labor market is *bad* per se, the left will not even give serious consideration to the damage that results from regulating wages excessively. The door simply slams shut. On other key questions there is much the same leftist reaction; so much so that those outside the pale have concluded the left's vaunted open-mindedness is a farce. The vaunted sifting and winnowing of all views for truth is nonexistent. A major body of Americans is so deeply obsessed with ideological imperatives that it is among the narrowest, most rigid group in the Republic. Liberals have abandoned liberalism and whore after ideological purity, which was once anathema to the very ideal of a liberal attitude. The fact that it is literally impossible even to discuss rationally a nonliberal reform with most liberals suggests that something akin to a psychic disease, some dogmatic inflexibility operates to shrivel the left.

The causes of such ironclad ideological virginity in leftist politics are mysterious and probably involve personal hang-ups. But from an empirical viewpoint, it can easily be demonstrated that the rigidity does exist, beginning in the moderate left and extending outward to the radical left with increasing potency. The farther leftward one goes, the more straitjacketed the minds, the more narrow the options for reform. Just, for example, try to get a leftist to consider the possible advantage of returning to a gold standard and gold coinage! (One reason such a standard is taboo is that it limits the power of the government to inflate its currency. It also increases private options and liberties to the extent that it circumscribes the government's monetary power.)

The politics of the left are corrupt not because they are rigidly collectivist but because they are an escape from self-discipline and self-development. The thrust of radical-left politics is toward the mystic goal of "the people." The major exception is the Black Panthers, whose training and doctrine seem as much devoted to paramilitary personal courage as toward tearing down the white machine. Predictably, leftist programs and issues will divert energy away from reforming the self: indeed, the Establishment the kids are so deeply alienated from is the Establishment of the ego. The reality is simple enough. The more a person accepts himself, the more readily he accepts the world around him. A hip kid, sodden with sex, pot, and porno, and full of the viciousness of Telegraph Avenue street people, and devoid of the hope of a comfortable income, or acceptance by the community, illiterate without the mastery of any profession; unaccomplished, with no authorship or achievement to rejoice over—such a person can only be filled with a self-loathing that transcends everything else in his personality and colors his views of everyone else. A man who cannibalizes his own soul and brims with disgust, contempt, bitterness, and ungovernable lust and folly, supposes that others are much the same, or if not, then that is all the more reason to hate them. If the impulse of liberal politics is, au fond, reactionary, the impulse of the kid cults and SDS politics is suicidal. The hunger of the radicals in Berkeley and Madison and The Village and elsewhere is to pull the rubble down upon themselves, to bury their tortured souls in their own excrement. It is as though hell expanded into the world. People who are subliminally aware that they are somehow berserk do everything they can to be caught and straitjacketed. They leave clues behind, and messages and invitations and pleas for help. The insane politics of the kid cults expresses this sort of desperation. This is not to suggest that the kids are insane—but rather, unable to govern their emotions, or, to put it into an older theological context, to cope with their sins. They are curiously objective about themselves. They see their own follies with the detached eye of the jaded and weary. This detachment

65

is a species of recovery of the self: it amounts to collecting the threads of rationality together again after a long trip. It is the same as the man who checks his pulse after gobbling sleeping pills to see if he is dead yet.

Perhaps that is why the radical politics are orgasmic rather than constant. A man with a deep intellectual and rational commitment to a reform pursues it with a constancy that is not apparent among kids. He begins by using persuasion: books, letters, magazine articles, speeches, interviews. He progresses to organization, with lobbies, petitions, and political planks. Finally, he shepherds the reform through its legislative obstacles. But the kids don't persuade; they rely on pure emotion, pure orgiastic excitement. That is, on building a high by drugs, acid rock, rhythm, and the keening voices of the young Hitlers until finally the trigger is pulled and there is a heady, boiling mass of action that explodes climactically into the target community or institution. It is not even emotional, but rather animal: the words are insignificant; what counts is the timbre and intensity of the haranguers. In this sense the kid politics are more barbaric than anything yet witnessed in the Republic. Of course, the result of some orgasms is new life, and perhaps that is a dynamic hunger among the scruffy ones. But their political orgasms are sterile; they are a rape upon a community that is not in season, and to date the radical movement has achieved nothing that could be called a reform. Not that the radicals wish reform. Their expressed political objective now is to destroy and profane all that exists, including themselves. They understand the link perfectly well: when they talk of ripping down the machine, the society, they know they are talking of their own doom, their literal and definite death both personally and as a movement. That is one of the things they see most clearly, and one of the reasons why their radicalism is the mask of the hangman; their cover story for suicide. And the poor, pathetic liberals who travel in the company of the dead are not aware of the grinning, macabre, doomsday masks around them. The liberals will not die grinning, but screaming.

The political exploitation of sex was one of the most innovative and brilliant approaches to revolution fostered by the kids. The Dirty Speech Movement that followed in the wake of Berkeley's Free Speech Movement was the awakening of the political possibilities of obscenity. The chanting of four-letter expletives was more than a verbal assault, more than an effort to portray man in a bestial light. It was an attack on religion.

The only institution that still condemns extramarital sex, obscenity, lewdness, and pornography, is the church. The secular state doesn't much care, although there are laws on the books limiting public sexual activities of various sorts, and some private activities as well. But the laws are dead

66

letters, in part because the Supreme Court has laid them to waste; in part because of liberal attitudes; and in part because the public is more titillated than repelled by the frank displays of sex in books, cinema, and elsewhere.

The church alone is the upholder of the old moral values of chastity and purity as personal and social norms. To be sure, many secular persons have been shocked by the public and communal sex of the hip kids and radicals, but the shock was an expression of community opinion rather than a deep moral commitment; of a vague, visceral belief in propriety and decorum rather than in an explicit commandment of God to contain human lust.

There is, of course, a dehumanizing aspect to four-letter words recognized among the sensitive secular people as well as the religious. To hurl obscenities at cops and governors and professors and politicians is to call them animals; bestial animals without that quality of spirit and intellect and character that elevates man from the plateau of the pigs. The use of chanted obscenities reflects heavily on the mentality of the kids themselves, depriving them of any understanding of the tenderness, love, joy, and spiritual beauty of conjugal love, and depriving them of understanding of why some men and women have sought chastity at great cost to their own unruly bodies and souls.

Chastity is a practice that forms the keystone of the arch of good character. Perhaps the Christian emphasis upon containing the most explosive of passions is based on the understanding of self-mastery. If a person can contain his sexuality, then he can easily contain his other lusts: avarice, jealousy, rage, pettiness, brutality—all these succumb easily to the inward will that has triumphed over the physical hunger for sex. That chaste male, in particular, must wrestle not with passive sexuality but an active, aggressive, dynamic one. Public displays of sex are explosively provocative to him. Consider, then, the impact of sex on militant politics, with as much lewdity or public display as will be tolerated at any given moment by authorities. The impact is orgiastic and extends far beyond sex. It becomes the crowbar to unravel the entire character. Make a man a servant of his lusts, and he will also be a servant of most other weaknesses—and leftist ideologues.

Thus, the destruction of character itself is the goal and result of the radical sexual politics on the left. It is worse than nihilistic politics. It is the triumph of Charles Manson-type humanity over the strong. For two millennia the church has interposed itself between man and his buried animalism. The result was always imperfect, and the majority were always backsliders. But even so, the man who chained his lusts became, paradoxically, a free and strong spirit able to concentrate on higher things.

And even in marriage, the lust was transmuted into something entirely different. It was sanctified as love, and through some special grace the man and woman who loved within the framework of marriage blessed by God were not the slaves of selfish passion, but communicants in mutual delight, adoration, and union.

Sexual politics, of course, lays waste to the whole idea of marriage, and again the state doesn't particularly care. The sex and marriage laws are dead letters. Marriage is also, at bottom, a religious act and law. For purely secular persons there is no particular point to it beyond providing a stable environment for the rearing of children. Sexual politics conveys the notion among the young and foolish that marriage is simply copulation sanctioned by the state, rather than a union of two spirits, two human characters.

Throughout Christian history sexual transgressions bulk larger than most other violations of the commandments. Perhaps this is because continence has always been the cornerstone of great character. The fascination with sex has concealed the reality that copulation for its own sake is a cheat. It cloys upon those who practice it most ambitiously. It bores because the partners consider each other bores; because they are strangers who have no intercourse except in bed. The world of the jaded becomes the world of walking genitals, devoid of intelligence, spirit, tenderness, and love.

In the end, the kids are cheating themselves of the richest earthly communion of all, and somehow they know it, and loathe the collar of lust around their necks. But it is the hallmark of this type of slavery that the enslaved are more interested in enslaving others than in freeing themselves. The slaves are also the recruiters, forever proselytizing among the young freshman virgins, for those who will surrender. The resistance is minuscule.

Slaves of sex, of course, are less likely to be free men in society, or retain any of the liberties bequeathed to them by their disciplined and devout forebears. The single stark reality at Berkeley and elsewhere has been the loss of the capacity to govern themselves. The mobs rush out to destroy the destroyable whenever some charismatic demon arouses them to public orgasm. The difference between mob orgasm and private sexual orgasm is less than appears. Indeed, the private surrender to promiscuity is the personal prelude to collectivist mobocracy by which a person lets himself be carried away by the rhetoric of the orgiasts screaming at him through bullhorns or high-decibel amplifiers. Even as the mobs who listened raptly to Adolph Hitler were orgiastic, so, too, are the mobs who listen to Eldridge Cleaver or Mario Savio or Peter Camejo. In purely revolutionary terms,

68

the move to sexualize radical politics, whether accidental or intentional was the shrewdest, most effective, explosive, and revolutionary device ever unleashed on American politics. And perhaps the world.

If the New Left poses a problem for capitalist America, it poses just as much of a problem for the Old Left, the doctrinaire, disciplined American wing of international communism. The logical and well-established strategy of the Old Left is to exploit native radicalism and discontent; to penetrate the leadership of the leftward groups; to heighten their grievances against the Establishment; and ultimately to enroll the dissident under the banners of the Marxist-Leninist revolution. Or, in the case of liberals or left-leaning intellectuals, to build front groups through which "respectable" persons can exert national influence.

None of these procedures seems to work with the young crazies. The prospect of Abbie Hoffman turning communist is about as unlikely as the prospect of Norman Vincent Peale joining the Dirty Speech Movement. There have been orthodox communists stirring the stew at Berkeley and elsewhere—Bettina Aptheker, for example—with some limited success. The crazies and their wild tumults, however, have, by and large, simply flowed around the disciplined orthodox communists. One might as well try to bridle and saddle King Kong as to ride the New Left. The brainless apes are not good material for the cadres of revolution. They are too orgiastic and unable to organize into units capable of sustained, long-haul revolution. If there are Communist generals, they are mostly running to keep up with the troops rather than leading the charge.

The radicals, however, are professed Marxists of some vague strain, but this collectivism is manifest more in a hatred of capitalism (they label any existing institution capitalistic) than in explicit Marxian utopian dialectics. If they hate private property, it is mainly because their weak characters have foreclosed the possibility of obtaining their own. (It is an unrecognized reality that even the most modest property ownership—such as a home or real estate—requires a perseverance and courage that orgiastic and weak revolutionaries rarely can muster within themselves.)

It is questionable whether the Communist party is doing any serious recruiting of New Left types. The party relishes the disorders and chaos and fosters that sort of thing at every hand. (Indeed, it may be the bagman that is enabling New Left leaders to zip around the country with such ease.) But the essential reality about the New Leftists is that they are not trustworthy and thus totally suspect in the eyes of any hard-nosed Soviet-oriented organizer. The party's apparent tactic now is to exploit the New Left—from a distance. To finance it, encourage it, foster Marxist ideals, unleash its destructive potential—but, by and large, avoid recruiting from it. Most of the New Leftists are too anarchistic to be reliable in any genuine revolutionary circumstance. The Black Panthers are more likely candidates for the Old Left than the crazy children of white liberals and lower middle-class squares.

But the New Left cannot be divorced from the broader global and strategic reality of international communism. It may be true that the young radicals are as contemptuous of the stodgy Red bureaucrats and grim Soviet life as they are of the institutions of the West. But the reality is that any weakening they achieve of American character and public policy amounts to a corresponding inflation of Soviet global power. If the United States collapses, the orthodox Communists, disciplined and powerful, stand to pick up the pieces, and not the rabble of Telegraph Avenue, or the hairy potmongers of the East Village. So deep is the isolationism of the liberals, and so absorbing is the inner agonizing of the rest of us, that the New Left is rarely viewed in the global rather than domestic context. It is fashionable to regard the New Left as frustrated kids responding to the injustices of capitalist America—and that is as far as the analysis goes. The strategic impact of the New Left in the context of the cold war goes unnoticed. The vogue now is for Americans to treat the world as if Soviet expansionism doesn't exist, as if there is no longer a Comintern of radical believers in well-honed cadres going about their daily task of turning the world upside down. Whittaker Chambers—quite a different breed of revolutionary in his time—wrote sadly in *Witness* that in abandoning the Communist Party, he was switching to the losing side. The kids are on the winning side, even if they are ultimately personal losers. Whatever rapprochement they work out with the tough Old Left, they will still be losers. Young radicals openly promoting radicalism don't exist behind the iron curtain. One senses that in the youth cults the Communists have discovered the perfect fool's army to march into the maw of resistance. All the hip children of the bourgeois citizens living sedately in the suburbs are the fodder of their war. If once there was a children's crusade to capture the Holy Land by playing on the sympathies of the infidels, today there is an altogether different sort of children's crusade, driven and exploited for malevolent and buried reasons that have a different sort of citadel as the target. The Communists have at long last discovered the highway into the heart of America. It doesn't involve any expansion of their reliable party; there is no point in that when legions of fools are on hand to destroy the Republic of their fathers like a plague of grasshoppers devouring fields of golden wheat.

6. ON INDIVIDUALISM

IN an era of heterodox culture cascading from the TV tube, the centralized wire services, and the salients of technology, it is terribly difficult to be different, and even more difficult to be an individual. The kids know it and search desperately for ways to express some uniqueness. Faculties know it, too, and go to elaborate lengths to build intellectual castles with turrets and sally ports rather different from any other structure of the mind. For many, achieving differentness is a kind of game that involves being forever in the vanguard of fashion: the instant a vogue achieves widespread success it is no longer palatable and the "individualist" must turn to something else just over the horizon. Some of the neoterics acquire a remarkable sixth sense that enables them to leap gracefully from vogue to vogue with a heady feeling that they are pacesetters and smashers of decaying icons. This is the frothy world of the mods and swingers, the perennial assailants of puritanism. But just behind, there are more substantial types who play the same game in the universities, advertising agencies, and belles lettres. Much of the cultism seems impelled by vanity. The neoterics want to be able to look in the mirror each dawn and see uniqueness there, not only of face but of soul and mind and personality. They place a high premium on spontaneity because it can never be quite duplicated by anyone else, least of all by those gray men who address others in measured words.

71

In earlier years the game was much easier to play because society had an inert core of values that one could achieve some disjunction toward. One could juxtapose one's self against Christianity, morals, ethics, patriotism, Babbitt hypocrisy, critics, evangelists, tycoons, or politicians. No more. The core of orthodoxy has eroded so badly that society lacks any organic center. The venerated things are gone. What was important about the group of liberals who wrote a new constitution in Santa Barbara a few years ago was not the oddities they came up with, but that they should presume to draft such a document at all. It suggests a profound disjunction with the past. It is significant that the old, redoubtable constitution no longer appeals to these men who so readily discard a tradition that has served so well so long.

But the point is, the social orthodoxy has vanished and with its evanescence it is terribly difficult to play the game of "against." The kids, in particular, often seem to line up against values and customs that vanished years ago. Against chrome in cars, even though chrome all but disappeared in the early sixties; against fascism, although it waned after World War II. (The kids who define fascism so loosely that it can mean almost anything will disagree. One of the ironies is that the word is applied now to old-fashioned libertarians like Barry Goldwater, whose object is not a total state, but to cut the power and the size of the state.) It is as if there aren't enough orthodoxies and fashions to oppose, so it is necessary to dredge up ancient ones.

Even so, the "differentness" vogues are bounded by carefully drawn lines that exclude a large body of endeavor. One is not considered individualistic for joining a monastic order, or for becoming a minister or priest or nun. Nor is one considered different for moving to the political right: only a leftward bent is considered "individualistic" or "different." Nor is one considered different by affirming transcendent values, or by adhering to a disciplined art form, or by writing melodic, rather than cacophonic, music. Differentness—at least as it is currently defined—must always be achieved on the side of anarchy in social affairs and disorder in the arts and literature. A different book now is not necessarily one that says something new and arresting, but one that is chaotic, full of typographic tricks and disjointed prose. A different book is one that demonstrates a breakdown of order, progression, and logic.

All this "differentness" is achieved for the sake of vanity, for the sake of being somehow at odds with the mass of men. Much of the scorn for bourgeois values and mores, and middle-class stability, is motivated not by serious philosophical disagreement with these things, but by the need to fly the banners of uniqueness. Those who attack the middle class are usually

72

refugees from that class seeking their own tenuous identities. It is a pathetic cult, and the tragedy of it is that the most stable and fruitful class in America is being victimized for the sake of its critics' vanity.

The game of alienation has deep roots in the liberal tradition. There is a romance in the vision of the man of truth pitted against the social milieu of ignorance and prejudice. So frequently has liberalism glorified the great dissenters, such as Oliver Wendell Holmes, that the very act of dissenting has grown to be at least as important as the fruit of dissension, which presumably is truth and goodness in the face of venality and evil. The dissenter is characterized as the bold, independent, farsighted man with a hunger for truth. There are certain corollary attitudes such as the belief that not much goodness or wisdom rests in the mass of men. Scholars, in particular, pine for the opportunity to be lonely martyrs. They take dissent as a mark of their superior intellect and their triumph over common sense. The academies actually foster an alienation toward the "outer world" of business and government which are regarded as direct threats to the free academic life. The academies also have fostered an alienation toward religion of all types and have questioned the motives, truth, and goodness of both clerics and congregations.

Dissent has actually reached shibboleth status: it is the god, the altar, the icon of the academic mind. One arrives at academic status not by building on the foundations of the giants but by debunking all predecessors, as well as colleagues and current schools of thought. In fact, the only discernible scholastic trend on any campus today is a unified skepticism-nihilism. Pure dissent. The dread word, if not devil word, on campus is conformity. One seeks to be anything—hophead, drunk, guru, or mad violinist—so long as that awful stigma of conformity doesn't adhere. Conformity to any standard revulses the bold, dissenting nonconformist who takes his dissension as the badge of individuality. Such people eye the world anxiously, forever alarmed that their views will achieve some slight popularity.

But conformity suggests there is something to conform to, and in a world of evanescent authority and declining veneration such pools of common belief are drying up. The elaborate quest for differentness, for uniqueness, for one's own little isle of alienation has successfully demolished the common social bonds, and has imperiled the social contract. Obsessive individualism of this sort simply brooks no agreement with any enduring norms. What is left is a fluid culture, vulnerable to bad, fuzzy about the simplest standards, and entirely atomistic. Everyone is his own nonconformist.

The irony of alienation is that it is still a binding relationship to others, and therefore ersatz individualism. If the world adopts your view, your mores, your interests, or your fashion, you are ipso facto a conformist and must abandon the ground you pioneered. Thus, your whole sense of unique individuality rests on a relationship with the rest of society. "Differentness" implies a relationship rather than an independence from others. Dissent is a relationship with orthodoxy, and the dissenter is as chained to orthodoxy as much as the conformist. Perhaps more so, because the conformist rarely makes a conscious effort to conform, while the dissenter agonizes constantly about his view vis-à-vis the "mass man's view."

There is, moreover, a mystique of dissent that belies the whole idea. For example, Norman Rockwell and Andrew Wyeth are virtually the only major artists in the country who focus a camera eye on their topics, each in his own way. But even though these are two lonely outposts of artistic realism in a sea of abstraction, pop art, and junk art, are they considered individualistic? Or the true dissenters? In pure mathematical terms they represent the tiniest minority of artists because they pursue techniques scorned by the whole art world. By all logic, they are dissenters. But the art world doesn't honor men whose discipline enables them to portray form and substance. Indeed, Rockwell is not even considered to be an artist at all, but an illustrator. This is not a defense of either man, but an effort to note that dissent as a cultural phenomenon applies only to those who deform reality.

If it were true that alienation is the key to individuality, then how explain Sir Winston Churchill? He was commonly acknowledged to be one of the towering individualists of our times; a man so unique upon the world stage that he was in a class by himself. Yet, Sir Winston was not at war with his society, nor was he even a dissenter, or an alienated man with a festering hatred of his people. On the contrary, Sir Winston was an advocate of nearly everything traditionally British, Western, Christian, and civilized. Repeatedly, he rose in Parliament to defend the wisdom of tradition: the capitalist free market system; the monarchy; the peerage to which he was born; the English custom of fair play; empire; the need for an open society. He drew upon England's genius; his pixy wit was marshaled in defense of the ancient ways. He assailed rampant experimentation. His every fiber was patriotic; he did not scorn nation-states, nor national sensitivities. He loved his island kingdom, his island people, and the sea power of his island people. When he attacked, the targets were usually the neoterics and socialists. In his entire career he scarcely ever challenged any norm, ethic, moral understanding, or manner of the English people, or of Christendom, or of the West. In short, he was a living rebuke to the liberalistic notion that individuality has anything to do with nonconformity and alienation.

74

Sir Winston was a man of devastating power. In Parliament, his foes dreaded his ripostes and sallies, and those who were foolish enough to joust with him were bested routinely. His command of English was masterful and he deployed words to evoke action, loyalty, and obedience. His individuality, then, had less to do with his differentness than with a powerful will. It is doubtful that any time in his long life he consciously worried about being a unique person. It is inconceivable that such a man would let himself be harried by such a vain problem. The world was too full of Mount Everests to be scaled for him to worry about whether he differed sufficiently from his fellow Englishmen. Winston Churchill achieved individuality not by rejecting his culture, but by embracing more of it than any other man of his times.

Individualism—the creed of nonconformity—is notably absent from Christian tradition, although individuals occupy a very high value in the Christian scheme. There is little Christian emphasis on the quest for individuality. Neither scripture nor the Christian ministry exhorts communicants "to go ye forth and be individuals." If anything, the goal of differentness is condemned in the New Testament as vanity. However, this is not to suggest that Christianity negates or devalues individuation. On the contrary, whatever uniqueness and character we possess as private persons is the fruit of Christian tradition. For it is single individuals who are to be the vessels of the kingdom of God. It is the individual who is the temple of God; the personal soul that forms part of the kingdom of God; and through the strivings of individuals to unite in love, voluntarily, the church is created. There is no formula in all Christendom for a collectivist redemption. Even the mystical body of Christ, in Roman Catholic theology, is formed from the souls of individuals. Each individual is Christ's vehicle: his striving to resist evil, overcome temptation, love his neighbors, abide in truth and faith, glorify God, is the chosen method of the Christian faith to advance God's will on earth. The Bible is rich with examples of individuals in their varied roles combining to advance the faith. St. Paul, in particular, describes the church as a body of individuals working according to their differing gifts: ministering, exhorting, teaching, giving, being hospitable.

As faith deepens in maturing men and women, so does individuation. Commitment to Christian moral norms supplies the communicant with an ability to resist wrong conduct. Thus, he becomes independent, and able to resist the suasions of the mass of men, and in this lie character and true individuality. Christianity also develops two other facets of individuality: obedience and humility. To do as commanded, and to do it voluntarily out of a pure commitment to God, requires strength of character. And to apply humility (honor to whom honor is due, custom to whom custom) is not to be subservient or cowardly, but to reverence things higher than one's self, which is the indispensable mark of maturity and realistic self-assessment.

The disciplining of the inner passions is a torment that few men willingly suffer. A man who seeks to live morally is occasionally desperate and despairing. One backslides. Yesterday's resolves only mercilessly pinpoint today's failure. The man or woman who would hammer his will upon the anvil of the Messiah will suffer temptations all of his life. The body makes its demands and these conflict with his spiritual man. It would be unbearable but for the knowledge that he has been forgiven for all things. Out of this hammering upon the heart there emerges through the years the beginnings of glory. The continuing cycle of transgressions, repentance, guilt, restitution, and triumph of the will over yet another weakness builds the special character of Christian man. He has triumphed over the fatalism of the Orient. At best, some things in his days are predestined, but all along he was free not only to build his will but also to apply it to glory or shame, or even to bury his gift like the servant in the parable who buried the talent rather than investing it for his master. It is tempting to argue that for all their obsessive search for differentness, the kids and their spiritual progenitors, the secular liberals, dread, even hate, authentic individuality hammered out upon the anvil of virtue and love, because the triumph of the will and of conscience over the will is achieved only in travail. It can be an agony and desolation that few men attempt, even though in the end when the trumpets sound, the inner will is bathed in glory and joy and nobility. It is patent that much of the secular world hunts for ersatz individuality; cheap substitutes for the triumph of the moral will. Their effort to clothe themselves in the rags of nonconformity or in the hippie garb of alienation is a flight from self-mastery. The same escapism prevails in the arts where the discipline of drawing a perfect foreshortened arm, or of hammering melody out of cacophony is so unbearably hard that form itself is assailed as a preposterous, limiting goal. The hunger for artistic freedom often reduces to a hatred of the unattainable; a contempt for that which is achieved only through the crucifixion of the spirit. There are only a handful who do not cop out and march behind the flags of the mods to formless tunes. Only form has meaning. Formlessness is nihilistic, a negation. The formless person is as much a negation as the formless art—a weak happenstance rather than the triumph of the inward spirit. Formless men and art are destined for the bonfire when more enlightened and disciplined generations examine us and our putrescent works of nonspirit and nonart and noncharacter. Rubbish! We have rubbished a generation of youth and have rubbished decades of music, art, and literature. We have even rubbished our sacred music: not for over two centuries has there been a composition in all Christendom to equal Handel's Messiah. Not for two centuries has any composer been so moved by his own creation, that seemed so in tune with the very angels, that he could exclaim in tears, as Handel did upon completing the Hallelujah Chorus, "I did think I did see all heaven before me and the great God himself." That which is touted as individualism these days is cheap crap. That which is hawked as artistic liberty and innovation is all rot. It has been a tragic eternity in the West since any artist looked up from his agony and saw God.

They call it alienation or nonconformity or individualism and all it actually is is flight into the darkness and all it accomplishes is terrifying loneliness outside the perimeter of community and communion. They have denied themselves the wine and bread, and in their arrogance they condemn themselves to a half-life of pawing through trash heaps. They are vain. Individualism is among the most pernicious vanities and, therefore, among the most pervasive sins. All that has been discovered by the giants of the past they are condemned to hunt for afresh in the trash heaps where the truths are not. They scorn what is known and revered, and in their scorn is self-destruction and futility. They have turned the Republic into a Greenwich Village and now there is scarcely a town safe from creeps and willies and bogeys. They opened a Pandora's box to let out every vile thing, and then strangled even hope. All in the name of vanity. They have devils; a thousand devils ride the shoulders of each bold dissenter, feeding his vanity, puffing his sick psyche, fostering still more assaults on the most venerated citadels of God.

What has obsessive nonconformity accomplished? Have the kid cults built hospitals, succored the poor, taught virtue or comforted the distressed? Rarely. A nonconformist is catering foremost to himself. He is not committed to anything other than uniqueness. One thing the cult has achieved is a grave weakening of the cement that holds communities together; the erosion of religion, faith, morals, love, and piety. The norms have deteriorated under constant assault from the academy and secular left and the result has been chaos. The only other result is upon each individualist, who grows self-centered, incapable of commitment to others, undisciplined, and in the end, arrogant. The nonconformist is happiest in a hall of mirrors, gazing at image upon image of himself. The noncomformist is Narcissus, rapt at poolside, forever infatuated with his skill is dissociating himself with newly discovered repressions or orthodoxies shared by the run of decent men. It is a sad narcissism with neither beginning nor end, nor victory. The bitch goddess of individualism waltzes forever just out of reach rather like her sister, the bitch goddess of hap-

77

piness, and those who pursue hardest are least able to keep up; least likely to find either individuality or happiness. It is a tragic, feckless, bootless quest for nothing more substantial than a mirror image.

Among the alienated there has arisen the cult of Jesus the Rebel—who died because he resisted the "conformists" of Israel. Such an interpretation of the life and teachings of Jesus is questionable if not outright absurd. If it is true he was a rebel, it was because he established standards of love, goodness, and faith that were unbearable to others, whereas the secular nonconformist is forever seeking to negate all standards of right conduct. But, in fact, Jesus was not a conscious political rebel seeking to overthrow Israel, or deliver the Jews from Rome, or, indeed, become any sort of secular king. He came, he said, to fulfill the law and prophesies of the past, and to restore the law which had been perverted by pharisaical fanaticism. He taught not revolution but the rendering unto Caesar of the things that are Caesar's. He was offered the revolutionary opportunity on his way to confrontation with the cross—the people sought to make him king. But he rejected that avenue. He urged those of lesser station to pay custom, honor, and tribute to those whom it was due—scarcely a revolutionary formula. He sought not only to validate the old law but also to supersede it with a new covenant between God and man. But there was no rebellion in all this. If He was a nonconformist, it is only in the sense that devout Christians ever since have been nonconformists: they reject the world, and adhere or conform, to the will of God. Jesus sought to dethrone no one, to topple no government, and to reform no social structure. He was not alienated from his people. To make a romantic nonconformist of Him is to deny His mission and undermine the conformity to God's will that was central to His teachings. At bottom, the myth of Jesus the Rebel founders on a key fact: the charges against Him were trumped up. He had never been a subversive. Pilate could find no wrong in Him.

The kids hunger to be different. Some grow great bushy beards and woolly hair to suggest differentness, but the extension of hair follicles several inches scarcely achieves that. Some wear love beads and fringed jackets and bizarre boots to be different, but unfortunately their naked bodies are altogether the same as everyone else's naked body. If they mature a little, they usually comprehend that there is no satisfaction in mere differentness. Superiority is more rewarding, and virtue is even more rewarding. Ultimately, obedience to God is the most rewarding, though it is very difficult for the kids to imagine any joy in any sort of obedience, even the obedience demanded by the Lord of Lords and King of Kings. This is the authoritarian viewpoint, they suppose, never comprehending, in their arrogance, that the veneration of just authority is at the root of civilized conduct, happiness, and individuation. The kids covertly hunger for something to revere, and have lately been reverencing the seamless web of nature and the life chain—but they don't suppose they are reverencing authority in that magnificent web of life, though, of course, they are. The authority of nature, long perverted and abused by many, has been rediscovered at last, perhaps by those who hunger the most for the authority of God. Indeed, some have begun to describe nature as God, which it is not, though it is a part of the works of God.

When they mature enough to see how similar they are; how commonly they share the problems, hopes, and antagonisms of all men, they blame it on mythical "authoritarians" in square society, rarely comprehending that parental and social authority are the molders of individuality. It is true that an undisciplined child can evolve into a spontaneous, personable adult; but it is also true that such an adult is likely to be rudderless, while the disciplined child acquires the rudder to set sail into a gale of trouble. The under-thirties have been victimized by several liberalistic vogues that boil down to permissiveness or parental unconcern. If it is true that God chastens whom he loves, so is it true that a parent chastens his beloved children, for their sake. Without chastening, there is little growth, and without growth, the independent adult never evolves, and there are only aging flower children.

One of the reasons the flower children kneel at the altar of an impossible morality is that they are secular and have little acquaintance with the word of God. Christian understanding, curiously enough, leads most believers away from a rigid, utopian morality that is utterly impossible to achieve on earth. The Christian education continually supplies lessons in ambiguity: the Prince of Peace smashing tables of money changers in the temple, for example, or David slaying Goliath without incurring the wrath of God. Scripture is a catalogue of sins and follies—and forgiveness and love. The child who has not been introduced to this vast panorama of moral striving and personal failure does not acquire the means to reconcile rigid ideals with daily experience. In Christianity is the great reconciliation between what we do as men and the ideal of perfect goodness and love.

Thus we arrive at one of the great paradoxes: the alien kids have put the more orthodox of their elders on trial. They are finger-pointers; they are stuffed with the debunking cynicism of their mentors, and they see Christianity not as a sublime force upon the stage of history that individualized generations of men, but rather as a force that produced only witch hangers. And yet these accusers are unquestionably tumultuous, narcissistic, undisciplined, and selfish. Even their most notable sallies into charity—Vista and the Peace Corps—don't involve anywhere near the self-sacrifice and surrender of self of any girl who ever entered a convent, or any young man who chooses the ministry.

What is worse, the kids simultaneously uphold a rigid and impossible morality, while denying the existence of moral standards. The whole structure of the New Morality is situational. That is, there are no objective moral standards, especially in sexual conduct, residing outside of one's self or imposed by recognized authority. A person is free to do his thing and has only his own subjective conscience as his guide. But while this is the moral code—or lack of code—he applies to himself and his under-thirty generation, he turns around and applies fanatical and impossible standards to his elders who, in his estimation should not be involved in war, in obtaining profit, or in material gain. The hypocrisy of the kids is total and astonishing because it runs so deep. Hypocrisy is the enemy of true individuality. A hypocrite is a man demon-driven to belie himself and his ideals.

This hypocrisy gives the kids a sort of half nelson on their elders, especially those secular elders who lack within themselves the mental mechanisms to resist the new morality. The parents have, all too often, conformed to objective standards because of social pressures or habit rather than from inner commitment. When secular parents are confronted with kids who reject standards, the parents have no defense and often secretly envy their precocious children for daring to do what they never dared to do in college. Enormous numbers of adults are secret allies of the wandering children; even those parents who fear drugs.

It is difficult to recollect even one among the great figures of history whose life-goal was individuality. One recollects saints whose purpose was to serve God, purge themselves of evil, and to flood others with love. One thinks of those who pursued excellence, achieving vast distinction because they composed sublime music, or painted magnificent portraits. One thinks of the pursuers of truth, wrestling against prejudice and evil. One thinks of the ones who have achieved power through statesmanship and idealism. One thinks of settlers and pioneers taming a wilderness. One thinks of all these people as vivid and distinctive individuals—and yet one cannot find one among them whose goal was specifically individuality or nonconformity. We know only a few angels by name.

7. LIBERALS AND KIDS

LIBERALS are far from being displeased with the youth cults, even though they chide the kids like Dutch uncles now and then for a few excesses. It pleases the older liberals to have a militant, ragtag army of revolutionaries to the left of themselves. Such a militant force has obvious political impact, and can be manipulated to promote liberal programs in Congress and liberal values in society. It is commonplace for liberals to suggest that revolution is imminent unless drastic (liberal) reforms are instituted at once. The radical kids are a handy bludgeon in the hands of leftist Machiavellians to frighten the nation into ever-accelerating social programs which just happen to be the pet liberal projects of the moment.

The kid cults receive splashy publicity: the drug and rock fests are probed and pinched, along with the kids' sexual freedom and radical politics. Rebellion, mayhem, confrontation are elaborately treated in the liberal press, but the broadening body of conservative theory and the ferment on the right are somehow ignored. One can properly assume that the liberal publications cover what intrigues them, but are silent about the alarming—and radically different—ideas being propounded by young conservatives.

The kid cults are, in large measure, the product of a disintegrated liberal cosmology, even though the kids in the end will rip free from their liberal mentors. Liberal issues dominate and inform the kid cults. At the center of the youth movement is Dissent for its own sake, nonconformity, hatred of authority—indeed, hatred of both state authority and the mild authority vested in tradition, custom, and religion. The kids, as their liberal elders, are pacifists where Vietnam is involved, usually hawkish where Israel is involved; opposed to the "military-industrial complex" (which is a code term for capitalism); in favor of free sexuality; in favor of extending free speech to physical acts of mayhem done in the name of politics; in favor of material and legal equality for blacks; in favor of interventionist economics; and inclined to believe patriotism and treason are outmoded and irrational. As with the liberals, the kids generally favor unstructured art and music; are smitten by the possibility of utopia through science; are inherently skeptical; devoid of religion, and inclined to reject community moral standards.

It has been with explicit encouragement from liberal faculty members that youth cults have blossomed like nightshade on innumerable campuses. Professors actively supported the Free Speech Movement and the subsequent uproars across the Republic, and only relatively recently have some of the more reflective liberal academicians begun to pull away from the antics performed in the name of free speech. Some such as Sidney Hook now denounce the cults as fascistic mayhem, or simple brat behavior, but these are a tiny minority. Most faculties are enthusiastic about the kid cults, and even adopt the externals themselves, grow beards, plot against campus and public authority, promote revolution and, in general, behave in a most unscholarly manner.

Numerous liberals secretly believe the kids are a renovative force that will smash the corruptions of their elders. Indeed, there are liberals who secretly have yearned to belong to the kid cults, but wouldn't dare because of the "repressive" forces hemming them in. Reich's *The Greening of America* is built around the idea that the young are a beautiful New Wave. It reveals a clear underlying utopian vision of a free, post-Christian society enjoying truth and beauty, and pure honesty in human relationships.

Tell a youthful revolutionary he should work within the flexible American system, and he will give you short shrift because the system is his target and reform is not his object. He has reversed the equation: reformist pressures are vehicles to use in destroying the system. The kids promote reform not to ameliorate some evil, but as a rationale for revolution. They seek to demonstrate that reform perforce must fail because the system is corrupt. It is rebellion that starts them salivating: dissent enlarged and glorified as the godhead of the whole youth movement. Most liberals are well aware of this, but nonetheless make alliances of convenience with the kids to enlarge the welfare state. The alliance delights and titillates the liberal soul, which harbors the notion the kids are pure dissenting innocents out to whip the hated orthodoxies into submission forever.

Liberal reformers set the stage for the kid-cult assault on the system by attacking it abrasively themselves for decades. Court decisions broadly expanded the modes of protest, knocked down most barriers to free speech, threw a mantle of holiness around extralegal activity so long as it was politically oriented, converted innumerable commonplace crimes, such as trespass, into valid behavior so long as politics and dissent were the motives; established a justice system that greatly increased the probability of escaping punishment; and weakened the force and majesty of law itself by insisting that it be freely altered by appointive courts rather than the nation's legislative bodies.

The kids accepted all this as a massive hunting license. If the liberals were cowardly when it came to acting out the logical consequences of their own ideology, the kids were not, and the nation has been under revolutionary siege ever since. The kids also inherited the liberal ambivalence toward the state; except that what was ambivalent in liberals is schizophrenic in the kids. Liberals are basically statists; virtually all of their reforms increase the power and authority of the bureaucracy. But liberals also ambush the state along the trails of the bill of rights. If they want commerce more rigorously controlled, and gun ownership more intensively regulated, and welfarism imposed coercively on all, they also want vast sexual liberties, and publishing freedom, immunity to the legal consequences of mayhem, a military so weakened that the Republic may fall like overripe fruit, and an internal police that functions more with valentines than with billy clubs. The kids, on the other hand, are anarchist and totalitarian—an impossible combination in rational men. They violently reject the state where it impinges on themselves, but for the rest of mankind, the hated capitalists especially, they propose deep collectivist programs and coercive control. Their "participatory democracy" is a cosmetic pseudonym for what they hope will be elective socialism, or denatured Marxism.

Along such a path lies madness. Wherever the state assumes ownership or control of men's livelihoods, it also assumes control over their persons. If the state (which ought never to be confused with the "people") is an employer and manager, or (in the fascist system) dictator of all the minutiae of operation, then the state has acquired deep control over the destinies of common men, including their working hours, wages, work conditions, employment opportunities, job transfers, moves from place to place, services, housing, entertainment, and even religion. The mass of men, of course, want some supervision in many of these areas, but would reject the degree of state penetration proposed by the young radicals. If it is true that the wretched ones behind the Iron Curtain hunger for more personal liberty it is also true that many persons in western democracies ache to have the government assume more responsibility over their welfare. The young radicals are in the vanguard of those who want more control.

The total state cannot tolerate—even for an instant—the sort of rebellion that erupts sporadically among the kid cultists in America. Such a chronic sedition would be wiped out ruthlessly by secret police and the penalty would be the firing squad and concentration camp. Conceivably there is a perverse hunger among the freewheeling kids for just such a firm retribution: communism may seem attractive to them because it does impose and enforce boundaries. It is, at least, an edifice that has structured social relationships, rather than an asylum of tolerance and endless accommodation. What the kids may find subtlely enticing about communism is not its highly touted benevolence toward the lesser and poorer souls, but rather its rigid structure that places everyone in a niche where there is no identity crisis at all. Once the kids vomit up their anarchy, they find Leviathan attractive and seductive.

Liberal doctrine upholds the ideal of a responsible state and rejects the old orthodoxy of the negative government that is best when it governs least. The commitment to intervention is massive: there is no facet of human distress that the reformist liberal impulse would not wish to heal through the medium of state power. So long as the welfare state remains under the aegis of democratically elected officials, according to liberal orthodoxy, there is minimal danger of corrupt, tyrannical regimentation.

State responsibility, rather than private freedom, then, is the keynote of most liberal politics (except for the civil libertarian corner). There is a continuing shift in a liberal régime away from personal options and personal responsibility. One no longer needs to save for rainy days or old age: the government does it for everyone. Less and less must a citizen suffer the consequences of his foolishness, or, conversely, reap the reward for his prudence. At every hand, the responsible state removes from him the necessity to regulate his existence, or in the deeper context, to be a man. It is ironic that the very doctrine that professes to free every man to reach his maximum potential is continually denying all men the very decision-making powers over their lives that enable them to mature.

From the older individualist viewpoint, all this transference of responsibility to government frustrates individuals, weakens the fiber of their manliness, and entices the most fruitful of men to the *dolce vita*. Individualists argue that unless people learn to cope with adversity and suffer the

84

consequences of folly, they never grow, any more than the overprotected child grows. That is not a rationale for heartlessness nor callous disregard for distress, but rather an understanding that work is good, and relief programs ought to encourage work. They argue, further, that the onerous tax load on individuals and businesses to pay for all the social responsibility is now so great that it discourages enterprise: the tax load itself is the primary cause of poverty, distress, and despair. The entrepreneur is harried at every turn not only by crushing taxes but also by paper work and capricious regulation from endless sets of local, state, and federal agencies. The individualists argue even more vehemently that to deprive individuals of responsibility for their welfare is to deprive life of its very meaning. Our sense of self, and growth, rests on our achievement of good character, inner strength, and virtue.

The orthodox Christian approach to social responsibility has been closer to the individualist one, although the thrust of Christianity has been primarily moral. The individual is charged with the necessity to act honorably to please God. Man is commanded to be diligent in business, to avoid sloth, to be generous in almsgiving. There is also, however, the event of the cross, through which the Christian not only pardons others but also is pardoned in turn, a theological point that has much to do with whether assistance to others is given cheerfully, or with a bookkeeping resentment. By and large, Christianity has not, until recently, sought to transfer social responsibility to the government, but rather has historically sought to maximize responsibility in its communicants and in the church itself. To this day, the church remains a major engine of charity and education in some countries. But many modern churchmen have acknowledged the liberal criticism of Christianity that it has failed to build the secular city; that it has been too pious and otherworldly to help the suffering masses; that, indeed, Christian doctrine is wholly inadequate to cope with the distress of the multitudes in an industrial state.

Thus, as usual, twentieth-century Christians have been forced to the defensive and liberalism appears to be occupying the moral high ground. The liberal criticism of the church is often couched in devastating language: the church is run by self-serving, pious Babbitts who are oblivious to suffering; who give little and care less; who ignore those of other races, and the festering slums in which they breed; who exploit the poor in business; whose charities—such as baskets of food for the poor on Christmas Day—make a mockery of the very idea of mercy when so many are living a grinding, desperate existence. The liberal criticism frankly suggests that the old Christian doctrine of personal responsibility is impractical and romantic. That the hungry masses cannot be cared for simply by applying Christian idealism to the mess. Liberals concede that the church achieved some noble things, such as building innumerable hospitals, but they argue that charity and medicine are too complex and costly to depend on the whims of church finance and voluntary donation. It is the realm of professionals. Some liberals conceded that the needy didn't starve prior to the New Deal: there were charitable mechanisms functioning, including the church, county poor farms, old age homes, and a great deal of personal giving. But they argue that standards have so risen since the days when charity was in the hands of local volunteers that it would be impossible to reconstitute the older, personalized charity. In any case, they argue, the Christian church is evanescent and likely to be engulfed in the wave of secularism and science.

Moreover, they contend that the church's doctrine of forgiveness undermines responsible resolve by individuals. The liberal forever has the monkey on his back; he is driven, even obsessed, with applying state solutions to every human misery as a way of expiating his own guilt. If he could, he would offer the benevolent state to the man who suffers from piles, ingrown toenails, and a sex hang-up as much as to the widow with ten kids and no resources. But the Christian, he argues, is too caught up in glorifying his God and the Son; too absorbed in what happens in the pews rather than on the streets. And worse, the Christian achieves forgiveness and is relieved of the pricks of conscience, and, therefore, does little or nothing about others. The concepts of heaven and hell are mythical spurs to force good conduct, but they don't seem to have much impact when it comes to drawing men away from their hellishness on earth, say the secular critics. So long as Christianity evades the here and now, it is an inferior moral doctrine.

Thus does the Christian church stand condemned at the bar of secular opinion as a morally inferior relic of the past. Christians can only reply that the business of the true church—as emphasized repeatedly by the Founder—is the winning of souls to God rather than the creation of a global charity. That is, the church is a religion; its first commitment is to spread the gospel of a loving and forgiving Lord to all nations. These are mysteries that a secular man cannot experience, or even fully grasp. Responsibility, then, in the Christian cosmology, can never fully rest with man; it is embedded in the will of God.

However, that doctrine is not a Christian cop-out. The church teaches a doctrine of deep responsibility and brotherhood. Unlike liberalism, which bases its meliorist hopes primarily on a transfer of responsibility away from individuals and local government to the federal government and the United Nations, the church creates responsibility in the breasts of believers, and charges them to care. The fact that few believers live up to the charge placed upon them does not mean the charitable thrust of Christianity is wrong, but that the ideal transcends the behavior of ordinary men. Christian charity is not separable from faith. Jesus reminded His followers that whatever they did unto the least of the little ones, they did also unto Him. Thus, He intertwined charity and faith into a unified teleology.

The kids, at bottom, are engaged in a massive transfer of responsibility away from themselves in the name of freedom. There are, of course, exceptions: the occasional VISTA or Peace Corps worker, the organized drives to pick up roadside litter, the dwindling numbers of square kids who willingly shoulder the workaday burdens of the world for the benefit of unemployed and unemployable kid cultists. But the radical libertarianism of the revolutionaries is aimed at piling an even greater burden on fruitful citizens. The kids' promotion of contraception and abortion is rooted, for example, in the evasion of responsibility for new life. The kids' evasion of the draft, even if the thrust is libertarian, is, at bottom, an evasion of responsibility to serve and protect this abundant, free nation. The kids' penchant for mayhem depends heavily on the responsibility of law enforcement agencies to avoid tragedy, and when tragedy occurs, such as at Kent State, the kids are enraged because their elders for once faltered, and responded savagely to the insults and brickbats hurled at them. The kids have extended college into a decade-long vacation with summer vacations within vacations, all at heavy cost to parents and taxpayers. At least among the youthful activists there is little effort to assume social responsibility, unless one supposes that revolutionary politics is a display of responsibility for troubled people. Not even the occasional soup kitchens and junk shops that appear in hippie communities begin to relieve the distress of the hip kids, or establish an economic base that overcomes their parasitism. Nor have the hip kids reimbursed society for the heavy costs of caring for dropouts, drug freaks, and young psychotics produced by their culture. The tax load for psychiatric, medical, and welfare care for the wayward youngsters is staggering, and a further drain on the responsible, fruitful, quiet citizens. *Hair* and *Oh, Calcutta!* are, perhaps, the only economic successes in the whole acid-rock culture, give or take a few rock groups, and even these sexpot musicals erode values including the puritan ethic that has fructified the Republic.

It may be argued that the kid cults at least have a politics of responsibility, but even this is debatable. If politics cease where force, coercion, and violence begin, then a significant portion of the activists are not engaged in politics. The Weathermen faction of Students for a Democratic Society (SDS) may operate, to some extent, within the realm of politics—as all revolutionary groups do—but their spectrum of behavior extends outward to mayhem and destruction. Within the legitimate political spectrum, however, there are innumerable activist groups promoting such "responsible" things as Vietnam peace, control of environmental degradation, elimination of poverty, improved court justice for the poor, and the expansion of certain civil liberties. Significantly, however, these political promotions all thrust toward making others behave responsibly. Businessmen are supposed to stop polluting; the President is supposed to stop the war; Congress is supposed to fund poverty programs. In this, the youth politics parallels the older liberal politics. The major concern of liberal politics is to force the bad guys, such as businessmen, to behave responsibly. But most liberals, who function in academies, consider themselves immune to the regulation they propose for others. Propose to them that they be fined for polluting truth, whenever they do so, and the howls about free speech would never cease. Yet they are perfectly willing that entrepreneurs be fined for polluting the environment. Liberals are fanatically hostile to any effort to bring their own conduct to the bar of responsibility. The shibboleths of academic freedom and free speech are regarded as inviolable, and the liberals wear them as an imperial mantle of social superiority. The results are manifest: the academies are the worst-governed institutions in America.

There are, of course, occasional liberal efforts to assume direct responsibility: a group of liberals might inaugurate a day-care center for working mothers. Or an occasional liberal doctor might donate medical service. But, by and large, those liberals who do engage in social service expect to be paid for it, and expect to act primarily as lobbyists to get the government involved in their pet projects. There is among them a tendency to forget that all the square and conservative people who daily climb into the harness and pull, are behaving responsibly and even supplying the liberals and the government with the tax base and economic surplus that enables reformers to conduct leveling experiments and distribute largesse. The liberal minister, so eager to allocate church funds to some poverty enterprise, perhaps forgets that all that money was donated by his weary, faithful, hard-working congregation who gave it without a murmur. (This is not to suggest they give enough, such as a full tithe, but rather to point out that the givers are unsung and unappreciated.)

A politics based mainly on forcing what one group considers responsible behavior upon others is doomed to corruption and that corruption is already deeply embedded in liberal ideology, and even more so in the kid cults. The more successful it is, the more coercive it is to others, and the

88

larger is the gang that exempts itself from the burdens to be imposed on all the rest of society. The touchstone of the kid cults, "do your own thing," is a slogan devoid of all responsibility to others, to the state, to God, and ultimately to self.

Much of the hippies' rebellion is directed toward the unbearable realization that they are corrupt within themselves, and that no matter how far they flee—to the ends of the earth, to the surrealistic universe of drugs—there is no escape. Equally unbearable is the knowledge that corruption is the human condition, that it threads through the lives of their parents, their governors, their magistrates, their ideals and programs, and the whole festering world. Their conscience refuses to be numbed; not by drugs, nor by sex, nor by heady rebellion. The conscience is there, a terrible rod of iron, and in their agony are the lashing and chastening of an angry and loving God whom they deny and fight and taunt. Their dilemma is, at bottom, moral, for only a moral man can begin to like himself and know that he is liked by God. It is true that God loves all creation, even the most miserable and ugly-spirited ones, but it is their special hell to be unable to accept that love or to know the presence of the Comforter who dries tears and puts the arm of love around the shoulders of the desperate, and also walks beside the lonely, and wipes the face of the feverish ones. That is hell. Conscience creates the only hell and heaven we know in mortal life, and errant kids are finding no respite from its blowtorch heat. The hip kids are wasting an irretrievable life; squandering each day and hour and minute in lunatic follies and terrors. Such a profligate waste of human life is unbearable to themselves and to others. Hip kids and Weathermen and flower children are terribly conscious of every tick of the clock, and at the stroke of midnight another day is lost beyond repeal. For them there is no Holy Spirit to call upon in moments of crisis; no Lord to venerate; nothing to worship. A man deprived of something to worship is deprived of the reason to be. For no man can know why he is here for three score years and ten, a free agent to do as he will, unless he knows his existence has some purpose.

They hate their corruptors who abound everywhere in secular society. They hate their alcoholic, divorced, and greedy parents. But they also hate their virtuous, devout, generous, and honorable parents, too. They hate the hip ministers who chuck out scripture and moral law in order to be more "relevant" to the corrupt, who hunger only for a rough, firm hand to yank them from their pits and cages. They hate the image-conscious politicians and those executives who have mastered the ways to milk the world. They hate the cynical newsmen and TV reporters who mount the

89

kids in their butterfly collections of clipping, or arrange for a kid or two to clobber a cop for the benefit of the networks. And they hate their liberal mentors who have seduced them into believing that the state is God.

If they know somehow they have been rubbished, they know also they were seduced into it, and much of their destructiveness is pure vengeance. If they are rubbished, then so shall the whole world be. No man is a nihilist. To live without belief and faith and meaningful love, and veneration, is more than the faltering spirit can endure. If they dismantle their world, it is because some deep racial instinct for survival overpowers them, and they are stamping their seducers with the mark of the beast, and with the abomination of desolation. If they are rubbished and their seducers have barred the way to the altars of Redemption, then the churches, too, shall be rubbished along with the other plastic and rubber of a rubbish society and a rubbish globe. They will carry their hell outward and flaunt it nakedly, and hang millstones around the necks of their corruptors and seducers and throw them into the same dark sea that floods heavily through their souls. The academies will drown. They think there is no turning back, but there is, at the feet of the One who cares.

But even as lilies grow in manure piles, so do some of the young acquire beauty and grace amidst the rubbishing of their generation. Among the best of the kids there is a fierce honesty and patience, and an earnest effort to love and understand. To grow up straight in the crooked world is a rare, beautiful achievement.

If strange doctrines erupt like toadstools among the dampened young, it is because their elders doubt. Liberals especially doubt not only the traditional American values such as the old individualism but also doubt their own doctrine. Secular men doubt not only the existence and love of God but also the efficacy of a religion that has seemed to make Jesus the exclusive property of white men and affluent nations. All this doubt is expressed in endless muckraking and debunking; in the classroom ridicule of the nation's most honorable men. It leaves, ultimately, a vacuum of faith on the campuses, into which rush all the absurdities of astrology, Marxism, witch cults, and all the other squalid and ignorant doctrines long since discarded by the enlightened West. Liberalism is organized doubt. The original thrust toward a positive value, such as private liberty, has given way to the goddess of Doubt, worshipped by professional Doubters and acolyte Skeptics. A young collegian can scarcely reach maturity without being taught about whole inventories of evil in the American tradition, and precious little about its strengths and foundations. In college the young person learns ultimately to reject his own society as something debased and corrupt, and under the royal thumb of the Babbitts. The student can major in any of the "humane" disciplines and plunge himself into a debunking milieu. If he majors in English, he will read novelists and essayists whose thrust is to ridicule their native land and its ideals. There will be more Sinclair Lewises and Hart Cranes on their reading lists than Willa Cathers. Most of the social and political sciences are given over to debunking alleged American myths, and especially the "myth" of the self-disciplined, courageous, enterprising American who is not only tough but also ethical and moral. Much of such instruction is not a conscious effort to impart liberal or secular values, or even a conscious effort to demolish whatever sense of patriotism and veneration the young person possesses when he matriculates. Rather, it is an attitude, a zietgeist, that has evolved in liberalism for half a century or more.

America-hatred is uniquely American, though there are overtones of it in England. American liberal scholars would be altogether perplexed if they were to emulate their French colleagues, who unashamedly preach the glories of France and take unabashed joy in the greatness of the French culture, tradition, and people. Even Britons glory in the genius of their island people, and in the explosion of brilliance which for five centuries has given the world its greatest men; its most magnificent generals, admirals, scientists, playwrights, entrepreneurs, novelists, essayists, and moralists. Such an unabashed joy in one's patrimony is not only lacking in the American academy, but a distinct liability for any academic who expresses such views, despite the vaunted academic freedom so roundly defended by every half-baked scholar. There are few academies that would even permit such an unabashed patriot to the ranks of tenured seniority.

A youngster can scarcely paddle through a liberal arts education without having every value he started with shredded by scholarly rippers. Those least affected by the debunkers are the ones entering the technical world of engineering, medicine, or the natural sciences. Those who are most deeply conditioned to the liberalism of demolition are the liberal arts and social science students. Obviously, most high schools do their bit to impart some appreciation of American values, or at least they analyze competing social systems and make the student aware of the troubles with them all. But that fair analysis is often absent in the college milieu.

The question here is whether such an education results in truth. If the faculties have imparted an accurate version of America, then they scarcely can be faulted for that, even if the truth leaves their students disillusioned and alienated. But in fact the students do not emerge with anything like a balanced assessment of their native land and its people, or its relationship to other world powers, or of God and religion. All too often the debunkers zero in not only on the hypocrisies threading through America but also on

91

the cardinal American values and ideals as well, leaving in the minds of their young disciples a landscape so ravaged and demolished that it appears to have been blasted by academic hydrogen bombs. The kids emerge really believing that the average middle-American is out to shoot professors, cut off freedom of speech, join the nearest fascist group, gouge everyone in trade, brutalize the blacks, and support wars of imperial aggression to line his pockets. The academics have foisted organized despair and cyncism on the young, whose minds have been seduced, if not raped, to believe that our great captains of industry are all crooked; our politicians are all corrupt, stupid, and immoral; our capitalist system is pure exploitation and chicanery; our defense of the free world is pure jingoism; that we are at fault in the cold war; that God was at best a motivating myth, but certainly not a Being to be considered by rational men; that Jesus Christ was simply the Jewish version of Apollo.

That sort of cynicism is all good clean academic fun. H. L. Mencken led the way through the twenties and thirties, and did it with brilliance and raucous humor. There was, and is, ample room for criticisms; that is not the point. The point is that older liberal generations did not have to earn their academic credentials by tearing apart our native land in an orgy of self-hatred. So long as they insist that America is the fruit of scoundrels, cheats, and immoralists, rather than the quiet, uneventful progress of innumerable honest and devout men, they will continue to warp the minds of the students they profess to enlighten. History does poorly at recording the fruits of the quiet, honest man. There is little grist for the historian or the social scientist in a whole lifetime of a farmer who grows his crops with the seasons and harvests the fruits of the good earth so that others may eat; or the daily labors of an accountant who surrenders decades of his life to the neat columns of figures that ultimately guide business into its crucial decisions. These are not the carrion for predatory historians, and when the quiet majority through history is ignored, so are the basic truths about the Republic. Part of the agony of the youngsters is that they have caught just enough of America's glory as to wonder about their teachers; to hunger for a return to the older, simpler days. There is a song they don't sing, though they all know it well: "Oh beautiful for spacious skies, for amber fields of grain; for purple mountains' majesty across the fruited plain. America, America, God shed His grace on thee; and crown thy good with brotherhood, from sea to shining sea." They don't sing that, they don't believe that. But they know it, and it gnaws at their hearts, rebuking their cynical young spirits. Their faces are always haunted. It is as if everything they had heard on their fathers' knee had turned out to be a lie. Their innocence is gone because they have been raped by the worldliest of men, and now they kneel at the feet of their rapists.

Listen to their folk songs and ballads: it is a lost innocence they celebrate. Consider their distrust of anyone over the continental divide of thirty—over thirty means corruption of adulthood. Their young cults may be corrupt in their own right, but they are shot through and through with hungers for a simpler, purer, more loving world, and ironically that world exists to a far greater degree than they know, or than their nefarious mentors know. Even while the kids emulate their corruptors, they love the past, love innocence, and often reveal innocence in their art and music, even against the backdrop of the dark and obscene. They listen to the Rolling Stones while their hearts hunger for orderly melody and harmony; while they search for something in Bach or Mozart. They call what they do dancing, but yearn for a waltz or minuet or gavotte. They take barbiturates to sleep but wish they could remember the lovely, tranquil prayer from Humperdinck's *Hansel and Gretel*—"Now I lay me down to sleep . . ." They need angels, even as we all need angels, and archangels and hymns, in times of trouble. They need a pastoral world governed by unquestioned authority of God, but they can find no God and no peace. Even amidst their debaucheries the hip artists yearn to paint ceilings in the Sistine Chapels of America, and do it for the glory of God. But they are seduced, and so the madonnas they don't paint become voluptuous nudes, and the sacred music they don't compose dissolves to acid rock, and the Handels among them become mad dogs. Never has a generation been stripped so drastically of its innocence, but never has a generation hungered so much to kneel before its Creator. To grow up, in their estimation, means to become corrupt, and so they remain perpetual children. But paradoxically, it is the dwindling community of upright and virtuous adults they hate most of all; the community that says nay to their free community of porno and drugs. Such people are lumped and dismissed as the middle class, although the kids are speaking less of an economic group than of a community that clings to older values, including simple patriotism, piety, religion, just authority, and continence. The poor Babbitts, under attack so vehemently for so long, have lost America. But with their departure from stage center, America has lost its most virtuous republican citizens who were her strength. For all the follies and fopperies of the Shriners, the foolery of the Babbitts, the struttings of the Legionnaires, they made a nation, and now they are all but gone.

8. TWO ISSUES

ECOLOGY

IN the ferment over a clean environment and a viable ecology there is a deep anticapitalist bias; a business hatred. In this aspect the ecology movement is not conservative. But in a deeper sense the discovery of a ravished environment and the struggle to abate pollution is a return to an older conservative stewardship concept in which there is a clear moral imperative to preserve rather than exploit; to place current industrial damage and needs in the perspective of the demands of past and future generations. There is also in ecology-awareness an appreciation of the blunt Christian prohibition against lust, greed, and material avarice. Christian teaching clearly suggests the wrongness of obsessive wealth-gathering and that injunction is directly translatable into an ecological understanding that material resources ought to be treated with some reverence as exhaustible supplies, and are not to be exploited to the last dollar.

There is a second undertone in the ecology movement: the belief that people—all people—are evil and dirty and that nature is the only cleansing force. The conservationist impulse is to treat wilderness as morally pure; humanity as corrupt. And the invasion of the last fastnesses of wilderness is viewed as the spread of corruption into the last God realms of America. The sudden adoration of the elk, deer, eagle, and alligator is based on the presumption of their moral innocence. Cities have become, in the eyes of the naturalists, centers of incarnate evil—not because their citizens are immoral or vicious or corrupt—but because they are people and, therefore, guilty of littering, eating, defecating, manufacturing, smoking, and occupying space that was once virgin land. The ecology-obsessed thus tacitly are posing a new version of original sin. By the same token, the naturalists suppose that a walk in the woods not merely lifts the spirits or creates joy when fresh air caresses the cheeks but is morally cathartic. The supposition is that a return to nature purges the soul of its evil and that in a wilderness the greedy are less grasping, the liars lie less, the robbers rob less, and the disturbed are tranquilized. Thus, the ecology movement has something of the aura of a moral crusade and its corollary movement—zero population growth—seems tacitly to suggest that the restoration of a virtuous society supposes a sharp diminution in the number of people; an increase in space per person. There are quasi-scientific experiments with territorial modes that suggest animals, at least, do need some territorial minimum to avoid stress. Whether man needs the same spatial milieu is yet to be determined.

There is profound good in the proliferating awareness of the rape of nature; in the renewal of understanding that man is an animal dependent on the unbroken life chain that stretches downward to the microscopic suborganisms. There is much value in awakening a public awareness to the imminent disruption of the life chain by pollutants or paving. That the air, the seas, the rivers, the oceans, the woods shall remain in a natural estate is one of the most hopeful enterprises upon which America has embarked. For whether or not there is moral signification in the wilderness, there are surely pleasure and practicality.

Ecology is one of those strange issues that have been co-opted by the New Left even though there is no rational basis in New Leftist dialectics for the worship and preservation of nature, or for allocating resources for abatement. For most of the young radicals it is just another convenient club to wallop the capitalists. But this thinking goes nowhere at all because each of the other broad forms of political economy—socialism and communism—wrestle with its own grave pollution. Indeed, capitalism alone seems to provide the margin of surplus and the incentive to proceed with costly abatement. In the communist countries abatement can be ordered by fiat, but the political directors of the state industries simply have higher priorities and the environment usually gets short shrift. Even so, the young radicals from Weathermen to New Left liberals issue routine ecological manifestoes, often copied ironically from such militant and wealthy capitalist groups as the Sierra Club or the National Wildlife Federation, whose lifeblood is supplied by corporate wealth. It is, indeed, the affluent rather than the very poor who benefit most from wilderness and who are leading the struggle for preservation and restoration of nature. It is only the relatively affluent who can even escape cities and penetrate the wilds. For the very poor, the blacks in particular, the whole ecology crisis is a strange and insignificant abstraction. Bad air and costly water may, indeed, affect them but they are scarcely aware of it; bad food and bad people and bad housing are much more palpable in their existence. The dutiful co-option of environmental issues by the youthful left suggests, in the end, not principled conviction but rather the ingestion of the old liberalism. Ecology is a liberal issue, at least in its regulatory sense, and, therefore, a New Leftist one. Liberalism may be dying but in its senescence it is still a lively exploiter of social grievances, hurts, crisis, calamities, and disasters that demand immediate attention in leftist teleology.

The Christian eyes the passions of the environmental pantheists with a mixture of sympathy and jaundice. There is a certain nonsense about the nature of man in the environmentalist viewpoint. The corrupt spirit will remain corrupt under the stars on a mountain top as in the bowels of the city. And the virtuous man will retain his virtue as much in his urban office as along a trout stream. The wilderness does, of course, rest the spirit, evoke a sense of reverence for the majesty of God's creation, and the genius of a Creator who fitted it all together and established this complex interrelationship of organisms. But it takes a person who confesses the existence of God to feel any reverence toward Him; for others there is only the pantheist understanding of a creation not made by man; the biological accident of the universe. The wilds can be restorative to health and spirits. This is well known and an honorable part of the environmentalist's wisdom. But the most dubious of the environmentalist beliefs is the supposition of redemption via wilderness. The mystique is that wilderness is the road to redemption and purification of man; nature being substituted for the cross of Christ. One must preserve nature pure from man's greed and wickedness and then immerse one's self in the purity and innocence of nature to emerge a cleansed, whole man. But alas, virtue does not reside in the woods, nor does virtue rest as a cloud on the mountain tops, or swirl in the icy clean waters of a trout stream. Nor does wickedness specifically reside on a slum street corner, nor in an urban apartment, nor in an urban hamburger stand. Nor can the soul or the spirit be cleansed without repentance and a commitment to do better. If there is no sacrifice, no catharsis in wilderness, neither is there a change in the personal spirit.

The message of the ecologists is that man can ignore nature and her claims only at his peril; that man is now at the margin of nature's tolerance; that further disruptions will produce calamities that will weaken and brutalize populations and ultimately deplete them and deplete the world's remaining mineral resources, wildlife, forests, and other supplies. The message is valid and is supported by the best probings of dispassionate scientists. The message also happens to dovetail with the liberal reforming impulse. The environment, manifestly, is something tangible and thus susceptible to state manipulation. Ecology is the ideal liberal "crisis" because it is mainly a technical dilemma; there are no human psyches with which to cope. The application of good yeoman liberal solutions ought to cure it; regulate the daylights out of industry; propose that areas x, y, and z be sequestered; start abatement proceedings, develop technologies, and we will all be one notch closer to the liberal millennium. Thus, the ecology issue seems quintessentially liberal, although it is not. There are deep conservative ramifications.

The late Joseph Wood Krutch observed that Judaism and Christianity arose not in a verdant, green, wet climate, but in a semi-arid and desert one. The Jews' land of milk and honey was Mediterranean and dry, a land of olives and palms and desert wildernesses. The desert, Krutch pointed out, has been the great incubator of religion. There is some mystery in the dry, searing, barren rocks and sand and cactus that has turned man's mind to transcendent things. The burning sun, perhaps, reminds one of the awesome power of God both to bless and to scorch His people. The desert was the place of retreat for the prophets, and to the desert Jesus repaired to be alone and commune with the Father. To the nature faddists, whose world rarely encompasses the barren desert but rather the verdant plains and forests, this is the only world we have, and they are obsessed with its preservation and restoration, almost as if the New Jerusalem were a clean river. But for the mystics who repaired to the secret fastnesses of the empty desert where so few things grow, this was not, and never will be, the only world we have. The ecologists argue that the very life systems, down to the air we breathe, are threatened; we must repent of our pollution or die. But the mystics and prophets for perhaps five millennia have argued that life consists of the spirit, and though the flesh may, indeed, fall away, the spirit is the essence.

LOVE

In scriptural prophesy is the prediction that in the last days the love of many will grow cold. If love falters among the mass of men, it won't be for

98

lack of interest in love. There is a secular and religious literature about love that is truly awesome in dimension. It is a common denominator in each of the cults and movements of our time. But the word and idea change meaning as they progress from kid-cult definitions through the liberal connotations to the conservative and ultimately religious understanding. There is a clear-cut division between the secular, which emphasizes sensual and sexual love, and the religious, which stresses spirit and commitment. According to all descriptions, love among the young pagans is orgasm, and the art of giving and receiving love hinges on achieving orgasm in others and self. Personality has little to do with love insofar as clinging to one another is the ultimate comfort and hope and release. Love is, among the young, interchangeable. The hippie families are communal; and where personality does intrude, there are temporary alliances that may assume the character of marriage and include children. It depends on the level of maturity in the young pagans. There is a difference between the idea "to love," which expresses an active participation in the beloved's well being, and "to be in love," which expresses a passive euphoria, or teenage gaiety upon the discovery of tender feelings. There are many who have been "in love"; but few who have loved. Under the liberal dispensation we have learned not to love our neighbors or fellow sufferers in life but to love the mass abstraction called humanity, or mankind. Nor to love God the Father expressly, but rather the godhead of liberalism itself. The thought of editorializing in behalf of starving Biafrans or Bengalis is more seductive to the liberal spirit than the thought of an actual visit to an actual shut-in to provide actual comfort for an actually lonely human neighbor. Liberalism is almost by definition love abstracted and rarified beyond personal commitment, to the point where liberals fondly believe and repeat that "all men are brothers," while they ignore their neighbors, or even more intimately, ignore their brothers, their spouses, and their children. Part of the thrust of freedom in contemporary liberalism is the freedom from personal responsibility toward others. If there is a benevolent engine of mercy, such as the United States government or the United Nations, then there is scarcely need for personal charity; and love becomes a sometime game between man and woman, a bauble floating on time, rather than a commitment, say, to rear children together, or support aged parents, or contribute to the church of God, or visit the spinster with multiple sclerosis down the street. The liberal's lack of love also manifests itself in permissiveness, which children interpret as a lack of parental interest in their well-being. Innate in the love of children is the disciplining of them; the rebuking of their follies and childish bar-

barisms. It is the unrebuked, unloved child who never matures or never discovers those boundaries that form the adult world. The model supplied to religious men is biblical; whom God loves He chastens. Even so, the child who is loved is chastised—not harshly nor viciously, but tenderly and always with the understanding that the punishment is to help the forming personality to mature.

Much of liberalism has been devoted to liberating us from love; devoted to substituting the state for community relationships, to smashing the moral understandings that have undergirded the nature of love as something outflowing rather than incoming. It is not easy for the weak to love. Nor is it easy for the amoral to love. Timidity, lack of confidence, inability to cope, all turn the spirit inward rather than outward toward others; and the weak creature conceives of love as a hunger—something to be gotten rather than given. To the extent that liberalism has eroded character, it has eroded love. Moral understanding illumines and guides love in a different way: morals are a conscious effort to avoid lust and greed, twin evils that breed selfish thinking, and an obsession with immediate gratifications. The deeply moral man is one who has learned to resist self-gratification, and thus to see beyond himself to the needs and hungers of others. A moral understanding itself is a sort of negative discipline upon the soul. The man who imprisons his passions is also imprisoning that pushy portion of the self that cares not at all for the well-being of others. In moral understanding are also rooted pride and the expiation of guilt, and these contribute to the self-love so necessary as the foundation of love of others. An immoralist can experience passion and tenderness and perhaps love for a while, but is rarely capable of the sustained, mature, year-in-and-year-out love that leads to a lifetime with one beloved, and children who grow to adulthood strong in parental guidance. Through all the webs of human relationship, there is the model of God's love to guide men. It is perhaps true, though unprovable, that the farther men drift from God the less they are able to love; or at least that the more lustful and less spiritual their affections, the cheaper is their coinage of love. But this is a most controversial point that is intuited by the religious rather than expressed dogmatically. The secular man boasts of making his way through life on his own, without the crutches of faith, and in this he develops a healthy self-esteem that may be the basis for a love of others. But typically the children of godless parents seem most weak and troubled; as if the first generation secularist had some sort of moral capital to expend while his children had only a feeling of senseless and purposeless existence that results in aimless smashing and copulating. Perhaps it takes a generation

100

or two before love, at least love informed by the Christian spirit, wanes into aimlessness. The tragedy of lust is that it doesn't involve whole persons; it binds only bodies and in the end the lustful person has simply united with other bodies on a sex assembly line. Love is a mass-produced cheap product without the differentiating experience of character. The Manson family was a love factory, with a dozen or two interchangeable parts. But there was no spiritual love there.

The difficult and perplexing reality of love is not that it involves heavy obligation—or to use the taboo word, duty. By all rights, duty ought not to be a part of it; after all, love should so inspire the relationship that there is never even any sense of duty. The duty to be faithful ought not to be a duty at all; the duty to support the beloved ought not to be a duty at all. The obligation to protect ought not to be an obligation. But these duties are there, nonetheless, and form the boundaries of mature love. They are there to guide lovers during the long gaps between ecstacy and spiritual closeness. We are changeable creatures; often despairing and lonely and rebellious even when we are secure in love, and it is precisely then that the love boundaries and obligations are most helpful. A rigorous divorce law, and a church that once frowned upon a casual divorce were not long ago formidable reminders that love has obligations. If we were perfect natures, we could love perfectly and all duty in the marital union and parenthood would be subsumed in the desire to please the beloved. But we are not perfect; indeed, the Christian supposes that with the weakening of moral restraints we are less perfect than in more faithful times, and that is when the obligations loom highest, either to be confronted or obeyed, or to be abandoned by weak personalities.

Woven all through modern life is the secular-liberal flight from the personal and intimate responsibilities, and therefore from love. Liberals pride themselves in their politics of love and concern, and have perennially assailed conservatives for promoting a coldness or even hatred among men. The intense ideological liberal even believes that conservatism is synonymous with hatred and callousness. The politics of love, indeed the politics that examines the plights of others and proposes political solutions for them, is the liberal modus operandi. There is no shortage of plights; no shortage of misery, and so liberalism has a boundless supply of objects for its compassion. The target of liberal love shifts from year to year, even month to month: one time it will be malnourished children in Mississippi; another, coal miners in Appalachia; another, the Chicanos and grape-pluckers; another, the Biafrans or ghetto blacks, or retarded children, or prison inmates or Indians. Often the original revelation of distress is the work of a crusading journalist or author: thereafter, a certain ritual obtains. Bills are introduced, the bureaucracy is urged to get into the work; the local regime that permitted the problem to fester is rebuked and threatened with a loss of power to a new federal force; the liberal press begins its polemic, often excellently done, to emphasize the muted pain and hopelessness of these objects of liberal love, and thence, with the passage of reform legislation the love objects fade from the liberals consciousness. "Something was done about them," in the view of the liberals, and love triumphed again over the callousness of the reactionaries.

But was it love; was it charity? And were those close at hand reactionary and callous? The scenario needs examination. One of the keys to understanding the liberal politics of love is distance. In a typical scenario only a handful of all organized liberals even meet the sufferers. The farther away the suffering personalities, the easier to love them. The closer they are, the more difficult and exacting is the problem. The blacks down south are conveniently removed from most northern liberals; but so, too, are the Puerto Ricans in the canyons of New York, or the southern rednecks who set up shop in Chicago. At a distance, any downtrodden people can be so conveniently saintly and lovable, and so conveniently assisted by an impersonal state. But close at hand, the deserving poor and oppressed seem somehow a bit less saintly. It is difficult to love even one's own family and friends without reservations; it is more difficult to love one's business acquaintances and the innumerable people we contact casually day by day. How, then, is it possible to explain the great outpourings of "love" for those whom the liberal has never met and would dislike and avoid instantly if thrown together? Would the typically literate New York liberal be able to form a bosom companionship with the Appalachian objects of his political attentions? Is he capable of spending the time of day with his Puerto Rican neighbors? How much has he in common with the Biafran kids whose bellies balloon from malnourishment? To what extent does he create a loving friendship with the union laborer whose side he usually espouses? Is his love grounded in palpable relationships with the living, breathing objects of his mercy, or is it rather an abstraction based on someone's crusading literature? Distance apparently is the sine qua non of liberal love politics. One would suppose that the liberal intellectual who really wished to love his fellow man would begin with his own neighbors and devote, nay invest, time, love, money, and spiritual empathy in those whom he knows and can actually help. There is an infinite supply of needy and unloved people in New York City alone, but how many liberals ever wander beyond the cocktail circuits of fellow intelligentsia? Distance is such a purifying factor; it makes love easy and cheap. It blurs complexities, so that all the local factors such as history, family problems, economic loading, local religious custom, vanish and all that remains is the vague lump of suffering that has been discovered by some sympathizer and trumpeted to the world. The liberal symphony plays yet another dirge and dolorous melody in the press, and the scenario begins. Where is love in all this? Loving must be something more than caring. Obviously, liberals care, or they wouldn't agitate for public recognition of the care-object. There is another phenomenon here worth remarking. The distant love-object usually is accompanied by an equally distant hate-object; the alleged oppressors and repressors, usually described as reactionary or conservative or parochial. But ought love also to invoke hate? If it is love that informs the liberal spirit, then from whence comes the hate? The capacity of love does not, in closer circumstances, limit itself only to the victims. Authentic love ought to be able to treat the victimizers with equal compassion, with the hope that a gentle education and rebuke will remedy wrongs. But that is not the way liberal love-hate of distant societies operates. There are distant villains such as "redneck southerners" who are supposedly the paradigms of all that is wicked in the south.

It is not correct to describe the liberal concern for its unmet beneficiaries as love. To do so cheapens an intimacy and interrelationship to the lowest, or most rarified, abstraction. In truth, liberals have nothing in common with the objects of their attention and would find any personal communion with most of them deadly dull if not exasperating because the victims reveal most of the attitudes of the alleged victimizers, and also most of the virtues and strengths of their oppressors. All of which is very confusing to liberal devil theories. The white hats get all mixed up with the black hats when any situation is examined intensively, and that is ideologically depressing. It complicates things when some grape pickers don't wish to be unionized and insist they are treated well; and some grape growers turn out to be sensitive and progressive people instead of Simon Legrees.

Conservatives are less likely to deal with abstractions such as poverty half a globe away, and more likely to express love only toward tangible people. But there are at least some on the Right who feel no responsibility toward others; they oppose the liberal welfare state but are interested in no other person's well-being beyond their families and themselves. These are exceptions, although liberal polemicists like to project the image of hard-hearted conservatism upon all right-wingers. The conservative vision of vastly reduced government does not include the elimination of local relief such as county poor farms, local charity, local welfare. Rather, it supposes that the reduction of the public sector would make more monies available to voluntary and church charity, and that such largesse could be distributed to the needy more efficiently and flexibly than bureaucracy can do it, and with more love. The advent of the New Deal did not herald the end of starvation and want; on the contrary, before the New Deal innumerable private and public ways were in existence by which care was provided for the needy and sick. The New Deal and its epigoni didn't suddenly put a halt to poverty; rather, they shifted the burden of care from the older middle class to the state, and the state has been expanding its responsibility ever since. There is less love in public charity now, but liberals would argue there is also more responsibility. One is entitled to welfare as a matter of right; no capricious standards such as the blackness of one's skin stand in the way of the welfare check.

Liberalism has never been motivated by love, but rather by political advantage and abstract ideology. At least the intent has been benevolent and responsible. There is, at one level of liberalism, some concern about the troubled, and even if the liberal mechanisms usually foist that concern onto an institutional machine structured to dole out mechanical tea and sympathy, that perhaps is the best sort of charity the secular mind can offer. The Peace Corps and VISTA programs were two additional mechanisms to enable the young progressives of sensitive conscience to deal directly with the poor at home and abroad, and however absurdly inefficient in terms of cost-performance the programs may be, they have created a few mature and fulfilled young people whose experience with the poor, whose joy in giving, has been a spiritual blessing imitating the Holy Spirit of those who have discovered Christian charity. Thus, however feebly, liberalism has made some timid attempts to reintroduce personal love into the welfare mechanism; to create counselors paid by the state to create the community destroyed by the state. Liberalism ought never to be chastised for its good intentions, but rather for its blindness; its incapacity to deal with whole persons and whole communities rather than just bellies or minds or eyes or fingers. Many of the alienated kids have had direct contact with the loveless liberal welfarism: their parents have been ousted by federal bulldozers in urban renewal areas; they have had their share of unemployment lines, unctuous social workers more interested in legal tangles than people; with social security checks and food stamps. This is largesse, tangibly and responsibly given by the state, and the kids know that, and support it. But there is no love in it; it is a pittance for the masses; bread from Caesar, even as the moon flights are Caesar's circuses for the poor. Moondust and surplus flour are today's public tranquilizers.

104

Charity motivated by pure love is a uniquely Christian enterprise and for centuries it was the work of unheralded saints, some of them of noble lineage. There is a place for love in the mass polis. More so than there is a place for impersonal welfare. VISTA and the Peace Corps do not really substitute for monastic orders, because they command no total sacrifice. It is a pity the monastic orders wither now, just when we need a vehicle for the sensitive ones to offer love to God and man.

9. THE TV GENERATION

THE first television generation has turned out to be revolutionary. At least a significant segment is convinced the nation is convulsed by crisis and oppressed by a grim Establishment bent on war. And if the actual revolutionaries are few, the soul brothers and sympathizers are many.

The kids' image of America is heavily negative; government, police, businessmen, and even academics are corrupt and vicious. Society is exploitative. Ranchers and farmers are ruining their land rather than preserving it for future generations. The blacks are cannon fodder, and rich men sit upon the pile of their corpses. Repression exists everywhere; there is a huge conspiracy of square people in the middle class to wipe out freedom. Business exists to produce shoddy goods at gouging prices, and to rape the environment. Those who profess higher standards are all hypocrites.

The dreary catalogue of America's sins is endless, and many of the kids believe it all, as a latter-day gospel. All of this is baffling to the middle-class squares, whose life has progressed smoothly, if not spectacularly, since the end of World War II and the Depression. The square perceives that he is earning radically more, even after inflation; lives in better housing; has vastly improved job security and retirement benefits; has some disposable income to add luster to life, such as vacations or skiing or boating; and he knows that he is free. He lives in an open society. He is free to leave if he chooses, change jobs at will, move where he wishes without obtaining state permission. His rising affluence is unquestioned: there is money now to get the kids started in life, provide some college, save a little. Taxes are high but not merciless, and if they are too rough, he can move to another state. He can read anything he chooses because there has never been more freedom to say and do what he will. His church remains free and untaxed, and no state snoop is recording in his black book the fact that he attends services. His life is tranquil behind the shield of American arms. No foreign invader threatens these shores. There is the bomb, but so far its use by any side has meant automatic destruction for both winners and losers.

He just can't understand how a land so free and generous, with stability and rising expectations everywhere, could produce a generation of haters, of kids who literally believe the Republic is a fascist-type tyranny, a police state, and an imperialist colonial power, and totally corrupt. His version of reality contrasts so starkly with that of the kids that the two defy synthesis.

That is, the temptation is to seek a still larger reality that incorporates both what the kids say about America and what the squares believe. Such an overview would suppose that both the alienated kids and the squares are right; that in this broad, vast land there are both fascist tyranny and the free world of the squares. But such a synthesis ought to be resisted as an intellectual scandal. The poles are too far apart. If there is truly terrible oppression abroad in the land, then where is the evidence: the concentration camps, the mass graves, the knock in the night, the political prisons, the state control of the press, the closure of the academies? The two versions of America cannot be reconciled by arguing that the nation has both good and evil; richness and poverty; and that the overriding truth lies somewhere in between what the kids think and what the squares think. One side has to be wrong.

The kids don't merely fantasize their viewpoint; they receive it from some authoritative source and that source appears to be primarily television or newspapers. It is conceivable that even though the media are relatively truthful and unbiased, the net impact of the style of reportage developed in recent decades could lead a viewer or reader to a version of America totally at odds with reality, and at odds with the one understood by those who are not alienated. The television world may be very different from what is actually happening. And the kids who absorbed TV with their pablum are not old enough to have matured when there was no TV camera to zoom in on every conceivable crisis and calamity not only in America but also across the whole world.

News is, by definition, nearly synonymous with trouble. When the *Queen Elizabeth* sails serenely from Southampton to New York, that is not news. But let her flounder and sink in an Atlantic gale and there are headlines and special TV reports with cameramen galore focusing on living tragedy.

The ubiquitous TV camera goes anywhere to record anything: militant Indians holed up at Wounded Knee; earthquake victims in Peru; a shanty that houses despairing, malnourished blacks in the Deep South. The whole world is the stage of television, and the diet of crisis not only grows with our technical ability to send images but also with the aggressiveness of newsmen in searching out the social warts and wens on the face of America. Where there is calamity, there is the newsman; and after him the editorialist to suggest more programs, more safety rules, more taxes, more government, or whatever, to "solve" the "crisis."

There is no longer any spatial isolation or localization of interest, thanks to the media. The TV viewer receives as his daily diet a mine disaster in Kentucky, an avalanche in Switzerland, a coup in Latin America, a DDT report from the Antarctic, as well as a few moments of coverage of his hometown friends and neighbors reported by sober men sitting behind desks. The result is that crisis has been democratized: no longer is a local crisis the center of conflict: one receives the local with the global and accepts both with the same aplomb. It was not always thus in pre-wireless days. A calamity abroad may well have been recorded in newspapers, but rarely with the intensity of local coverage. Thus, the kids are the first generation to perceive distant calamity as vividly as they perceive local calamity. Evil is everywhere, and the ubiquitous TV camera is everywhere recording it, often with muckraking intent. Much of what passes for news is actually an effort to rake up mud and probe it visually. It is the old crusading journalism in modern dress, but with the vaster impact of cameras and sound to make the wounds fester even more than they actually may be.

What the media fail to report, because it is not considered to be news, is the smooth, free workaday world of so many Americans—a world in which there are few crises, although each person in it may have his share of personal grief. Such a world is hard even to define, much less build into a plausible explanation of why TV news coverage adds up to a lie. We catch glimpses of it occasionally on the financial pages, where so many companies routinely report record earnings and dividends—little signals that all is well. Or sometimes, on the society pages, we are permitted for a moment to look into that other life, when we see a picture of a couple celebrating their golden wedding anniversary, their aged faces gentled by time, and serene after half a century of peaceful union of soul and body. One can find it in the corner tavern, where neighbors gather happily evenings for a beer and some TV and peanuts. Sometimes, it is visible in the procession of school kids trudging to class with their books underarm, just the way their big brothers and sisters did, and their parents, and the generations before—learning in an undisturbed, routine way the civilized values that pass from fathers to sons through the span of civilization.

We sense it in other ways: we know of products that perform well through their long lifetimes. Old reliables among the stores we patronize. Friends who have an inner strength that they share with others. Happy kids. Pleasant evenings of bridge and gossip. The vigor and outreach of an astonishing number of churches. The kindnesses of capitalists: across the country payrolls are burdened with unproductive people—the deranged, or injured, or emotionally unstable—who are kept on because of the generosity of an employer. All these things are not news, but rather the natural phenomena of a functioning civilization. We don't see them on the TV tubes, or written up extensively in the journals. And even if they were written up, or filmed, or turned somehow into grist for the media, we would still scarcely be aware of these realities because our minds are attuned to sensationalism, disasters, and mayhem. When a Middle American reads the black banners and views the evening news, it is often with a sense of puzzlement because what he sees and hears doesn't jibe with what he knows about life. What he sees is war and corruption and evil, or the umpteenth documentary on racial trouble in the South. The adult viewer has lived long enough to put the news into perspective; to understand that, at best, reportage covers only some of life. But the kids, in their tender years, think they see all of reality, and that reality is terrible.

Muckraking journalism creates its own reality, and that reality is surrealistic. The muckraker has infinite numbers of "problems" at his disposal because this is a world of sorrows. He moves from one problem to another, throwing his merciless floodlight into every nook and cranny with reforming zeal. The language often remains objective but the intent always shines through his work. He congratulates himself for forcing the blind to see life's underbelly, scarcely realizing that he is blinding himself and others to life's beauties and joys and honors. So deep is this muckraking instinct ingrained in American journalism that most reporters suppose that any reportage of the triumph of the good would prostitute their craft. Cumulatively, the muckrakers paint a gloomy portrait of man and his institutions, and viewers are led to believe that society is corrupt beyond repair. There is feedback, of course. The hairy revolutionaries repel viewers; the umpteenth documentary about prejudice simply turns the viewers off. But despite the fact that TV audiences are jaded and inured to what they see, they still have no other source of information, no reality-perception, to correct what the broadcasters twist, and the reporters fail to cover. So in the end, viewers and readers are suspicious of what they see, but unable to say why, or to counterpose another perspective of the real

110

world. The kids in particular have no way to resist alarums and excursions of the broadcasters—and so the TV generation is twisted worst of all. At bottom, the things that aren't news in each of our lives are far more important to our understanding of reality than the things that are.

The tube is a great educator. The kids' heads are stuffed with more facts than ever, but time and spatial relationships are lost. The kids get hung up by any world event. Apartheid in South Africa is as real to them as the mother on welfare down the block. There are no spatial priorities, no national priorities. If the Bantu or Yemeni are suffering, then to hell with the United States and its affluence. If the untouchables can't get enough to eat, then we must aid them. TV creates not only a democracy of space but also a democracy of culture. The camera doesn't distinguish between free civilizations and slave; communist or capitalist; imperial or colonial. If anything, TV gives the impression that most of the world's grief burdens men on this side of the iron curtain.

Even though the kids may be more intensely aware of the sufferings of Biafrans than they are of the elderly polio victim down the street, their awareness is abstract and so is their response. The TV world is ephemeral—passing images at the supper hour that fade as fast as they are seen. The Biafrans aren't quite real, even though the TV camera focuses on their starvation-distended bellies. The kids' universe is upended: things half a globe away have the same impact on the TV tube as things next door. The impact of TV on the psyche is as profound as the impact of the discovery that the universe does not rotate around the earth, but rather that the earth rotates around a small star in a vast sea of space. The human psyche orders its impressions and priorities in a pre-Copernican fashion, with all events revolving around the self, and the events farthest away of least importance. TV has changed all that.

It was the kids who staged the first "happenings"— pseudo-events that mock reality and meaning. Part of the fun was pure spontaneity. No one could know what bizarre occurrence might develop. But, perhaps, the happenings were also a way of thumbing a nose at a disordered world and all the categories of knowledge. A happening has the quality of anarchy, and anarchy is all that makes sense when order and hierarchy break down. The kids have no structural vision of life. No religion informs them about faith, virtue, and character. No patriotism or allegiance informs them that events close at hand have more relevance to themselves. Without a spiritual infrastructure there are only random mayhem, spontaneous combustion, and the lunacy of a universe without meaning. Happenings were an expression of that inner disorder, a disorder wrought in some measure by perverse media.

111

10. THE REFORMING OBSESSION

HISTORY is the charnel house of reform. One can scarcely think of any reform of the last century that has endured without causing grave new problems unanticipated by the reformers. Most reforms falter rapidly, or turn out to be ineffectual, or produce a result quite the opposite of what was intended. Prohibitionists believed that the elimination of John Barleycorn and saloons would usher in an era of public virtue, the end of family tragedy and personal disaster, and a world given to a higher way of life. Instead, Prohibition produced Al Capone. The proponents of urban renewal argued that people plucked from slums and placed in decent surroundings would become good citizens rather than welfare cases. They enacted a law they hoped would tear down slums and firetraps and replaced them with good, low-income housing. But, in fact, the program took an unanticipated turn; it demolished vastly more low-income housing than it built; it shredded and disrupted comfortable, cohesive old neighborhoods; ejected Negroes from the renewal area, and put innumerable small shopkeepers out of business. All of that occurred in stark contrast to the good intentions of the reformers. Social security originally was sold to the nation as a supplement to private pensions and a way to eliminate local welfare and relief. More recently, the poverty programs were promoted as a massive assault on the poverty cycle that trapped the subeducated poor on the welfare rolls. But the program has scarcely made a dent on poverty, except to pad the wallets

113

of an army of bureaucrats, and the tackiest problems of poverty—such as employment for low IQ persons—remain unresolved. The programs are now more vehicles for revolutionary activism—contrary to the express intent of Congressional reformers—than they are a helping hand for the needy. Precious little poverty money actually reaches the poor, although an incredible amount is consumed in plans, reports, and programs for liberating the poor according to the best bureaucratic tradition.

Proponents of the income tax once supposed that it would gradually eliminate the very rich classes altogether and close the gap between opulence and misery. It did nothing of the sort, and in some ways rests most heavily on the lower middle class which can afford it the least. Reformers always have chipped away at the armaments industry (or now, the military-industrial complex) as the cause of war—and war continues. Antigun lobbyists push for stricter controls—even as the hand gun crime rate climbs in areas where all good citizens have registered or surrendered their arms. Minimum wage proponents scarcely anticipated that their reform would shrink the number of available jobs, especially for black youths. England's Fabians scarcely imagined that the enactment of socialized medicine would fill the surgeries of England with malingerers and hypochondriacs, or cause a substantial portion of British doctors to emigrate.

The catalogue of reforms gone awry is endless and a commentary on the boundless faith people have in the capacity of political institutions to abolish problems. The rhetoric of politics is not amelioration, but abolition. For some reason, rational prudence and skepticism flee in some people when they describe the anticipated results of a proposed reform. When the reforms don't work out as anticipated, there is no shortage of devil theories to explain the disaster, or the higher cost, or the fact that poverty increased rather than decreased. The commonplace one is that nefarious lobbyists and private interests tampered with the virgin purity of the reform bill and altered its thrust; or the seniority system in Congress twisted and defeated parts of it; or the bureaucrats applied it stupidly and selectively. In other words, the reformers rarely admit that the reform itself may have been faulty or ill-conceived; rather, they lay the blame—if they elect to recognize blame—on the perversity of everyone else who had anything to do with drafting and administering and funding the program. But the one thing they don't blame is original sin, nor do they ever blame a natural limitation of what government—even the best government—can accomplish.

The thing I wish to treat here is not the efficacy of reform, but the obsession of secular liberals for reform—an obsession that overwhelms all prudence, fact, and reason. Even more than reform, the liberals are aflame with a vision of worldly progress: next year's government will be better than this one if illumined by the lamps of the left; next year's society will be more just, more compassionate, more rational if liberal opinion makers are free to exercise their reforms. It were as if the idea of biological evolution through epochs and millennia were sharply compressed by the left into social meliorism that will advance in seven league boots through the lifetimes of living liberals.

That there are movement, flux, and change is undeniable. That it could be defined as progress in the main, or evolution of society as something superior to yesterday's or last week's or last century's is a question so vexing that only a committed secular liberal would dare affirm it. There are a knowledge explosion and technology explosion and radical advances in information storage and recall; yet is there a comparable moral, ethical, or spiritual explosion? Is liberty advancing? Is government more just? Are people one whit happier? Is crime declining as it should, according to liberal theory, with the advancement of affluence? The case for progress, for an evolutionary development of society is shaky at best, and perhaps monstrous if the twentieth century is remembered as the era of Hitler and Stalin, the total states that penetrated more barbarously into the privacies of citizens than ever before in modern history. Not even the great, rickety, tax-obsessed monarchies such as that of Louis XIV approached in sheer terror the gestapo or the Cheka or MVD. And yet somehow, the obsessed liberals still reconcile all these calamities with an inevitable Progress, a sort of berserk Couéism of politics.

One might well inquire why it is so necessary to believe in Progress even as the world collapses. Ironically, if there has been progress, it has been bestowed not by governments but by alert business entrepreneurs whom the liberals generally detest. It was not governments that erected supermarkets and stocked them with an inconceivable array of spices and foods from the four quarters of the globe, an array that transcends the wildest improbabilities of an Oriental bazaar. Not governments that evolved the affluent life: dishwashers, fine cars, phonographs that could realistically reproduce the masters, fine entertainments, TV, movies, restaurants. All of these things are the fruits of questing private entrepreneurs in search of profits in a nation where they are still reasonably free to please the insatiable consumer. It is precisely in this realm—rather than the world of government—that there has been the most obvious and pleasant progress toward amenities for the mass of men. And it is precisely in this realm that liberals are least evident. If anything, many on the liberal left, somehow, resent the breakthrough that spreads comforts and the arts to all, in a market economy. The affluence was not ordained by the state. It did not evolve as the master plan of some pro bono society such as the Brookings Institution. All this gain was not factored into the economy by liberal choirmasters.

Yet, if there were progress, it is because the market economy is dragging the liberals screaming into the twentieth century and its miracle of industrial organization. If there were progress, it is because the market economy, in private hands, is so miraculously strong that it has weathered the incredible burdens of taxation, regulation, and harassment imposed by liberal busybodies. Everywhere where liberals have established themselves as preeminent—government and policymaking and politics—there is national disaster; but everywhere that business has been allowed to function unimpeded, there has been progress toward widespread abundance. Everywhere the liberals predominate there is not visible progress but rather visible decay: theater, music, literature, the academy, the government, in urban areas, on the East Coast. In all these areas there are mounting barbarism, crudity in art, loss of sensitivity, loss of public safety, increasing unrest, bestiality, criminals who pillage in the night. The progressives are confronted starkly by the decay of their own houses; it is in the nonliberal realms of society, in the countryside, in industry, in some conservative or religious areas of the country, that the nation remains most viable.

The questions which liberals rarely ask themselves are these: Is society decaying? Why? Do liberal-progressive programs and theories contribute to the decay? Does future progress lie with the enemies of liberalism? Has reform worked? Is big government the true solution? Wherever collectivism has been instituted, has it lived up to expectations? Has it solved the basic problems of those societies? Is liberalism valid? Are liberals happier, more productive, more honorable?

The questions strike too deeply; and, as a result, liberals prefer to blame devils than to face themselves. They run out of devils when confronted with the failures of programs that were conceived, legislated, and staffed by liberal shock troops. Most of today's liberals need a bête noire in their closet to maintain some sort of rational view toward their own ideology.

Reform is the secular man's god; his comforter, his hope, his salvation. Social progress is the cross and redemption. If reform, which takes the shape of social engineering or the Big Brother state, should produce perverse results or unleash totalitarian regimes, then the secular man is confronted with an agonizing reality that necessitates conjuring up still more devils and hatreds. The secular man lives in the here and now; he shares no hope in a hereafter. So his millennium must be accomplished in his lifetime. That, perhaps, is why he is so fond of repeating that the world is changing rapidly, even by quantum jumps. But it is never clear whether this is a wish or an observation. It is rather more likely to be a wish, given the perverse, constant, and unresponsive nature of the human creature. Obviously, some reform works: otherwise all reformers, liberal and conservative, would be laboring in the vineyards of madness. Whether reform reforms is not the question but rather what costs and penalties there are, and whether a bit of progress is attained in one realm only by penalizing progress in several other realms. There is, especially, the question of whether the alleged reform invades the intangibles so necessary for happiness: freedom, independence, and the exercise of personal mature judgment. A compulsory social security system, for example, pays benevolences and guarantees a pittance for the retired—but it undeniably deprives citizens of their privilege to achieve old age security their own way, perhaps by investing the money in stocks or in a business. These intangibles, such as the joy of achieving independent means to handle retirement, are not elements in the blueprints of the social planners, and yet they have much to do with happiness, joy in achievement, and independence.

Reformers are skeptical of voluntary and privately initiated benevolences which rest on the acquiescensce of those to be reformed, and the voluntary contributions of the participants. While these pro bono groups are not discounted in the secular scheme of progress, they are believed, nonetheless, to lack the power of government. In fact, the usual role of the liberal pro bono group is the instruction of the state about its future role. Even the liberal church is expected to be a sort of super pro bono group and not exhibit any power of its own, other than its moral wisdom. The state is puissant and thus the only true tool of progress. It is obvious that if the state's coercive powers are the reformer's hammer and saw, then the state must be the captive of the reformers, and must perforce expand with reform. By some semantical quirk, any diminution of the state and its power is not regarded by liberals as a reform, but rather as a step to the rear.

A secular reformer is a man who knowingly or unknowingly has abandoned God. The state is his god because the state alone contains the power to change things, in his estimation. He is a compulsive reformer because reform is the only goal that seems to justify life. Politics, the external juggling and bending and inhibiting of the power structure and society, holds the only key to the only heaven he can imagine, and if the St. Peters who sit as committee chairmen by virtue of seniority in Congress are impeding reform, or access to heaven on earth, then the St. Peters must be cast out so that all men, worthy and unworthy, can march through the pearly gates.

Secular liberals regard the church in a most curious and interesting light:

117

the church has failed. It now must come up immediately with radical new reforms to make Christianity relevant to current needs. It must plunge into social programs, and if the old-fashioned sin and salvation ideas are never again mentioned, all the better. It must move from cold piety into the secular city and lead reformers by pressing for more government service, higher taxes, sensitivity to the poor, and brotherhood. In short, the secular man treats the institutional church precisely within the secular cosmology, as the best of pro bono groups rather than as a religion. A goodly number of clergymen are seduced by the idea. But this formulation ignores the two millennia of reform already achieved by the church and ignores the central reforming and redeeming thrust of the church. The church does not usually reform institutions. Jesus had that opportunity when he was pressed to be king of the Jews, and he flatly rejected it. Rather, Jesus and the church reform individual souls, and the success of this effort is measured in the number of honest, honorable, charitable Christians who are injected into a thieving world. The power of God on earth is manifest in the Christian's ability to down temptation; to be merciful; to avoid greed; to place some emotional distance between self and secular passions; to regard the world in the broader perspective of afterlife, where suffering and achievement all have their reward, and evil will merit evil. The city of God on earth lives not in law or public reform or government, but in the hearts of believers. Any effort to make the church more relevant by urging it to promote (liberal) secular reforms is, at bottom, a type of apostasy. The apotheosis of the state is the principal reality of secular liberalism even though liberals will end up hating their public god. To suggest that the church play the role of handmaiden to this secular god is to suggest the church turn to a modern idolatry.

Liberals will propose new reforms of public institutions even if each previous reform were demonstrably a flop because the reforming impulse is their own private salvation. Each liberal is a frustrated author of benevolence. The attraction of communism to the leftist mentality is that it abolishes the devils of private perversity; it is the pure triumph of the state; the god reigneth almighty, and no evil spirits—greedy industrialists or rapacious bankers—can impede the state in its godly progress. There is scarcely a liberal extant who does not wish for the power inherent in a Communist régime—the secular power to do good, to energize reforms, and to impose radical changes upon the economy; the power, also, to make all citizens and subjects criminals.

For a Christian, the material world is always a moral enemy—the place of greed, vice, and carnality. But while he rejects ''the world'' in that sense, he still lives in it and establishes himself as a member of a concurrent City of God, composed of believers. If the Kingdom of Heaven were established on a terrestrial basis, it will not be through the benevolent state, or through progressive politics, or by making just laws, or by establishing the godhead in the United Nations, but rather in a community which has withdrawn from, and cannot be governed by, secular powers. That is the true radicalism of Jesus Christ. He was abhorred by the ancient Jewish governors not because He sought to overthrow them and establish Himself as a great reformer of Israel—but because He rendered them, and their regimes, unnecessary. A committed Christian has little need to be governed by extensive coercions. Jesus was creating a spiritual kingdom within a secular one, and the spiritual one planned no coup, no power politics, no treasons, no rejection of public law or public authority. His kingdom was maddeningly immune to the beck and call of public governors, whether Jewish pharisees or Roman procurators. The triumph of Jesus is, in a large sense, a triumph over the state and over the future totalitarian state. The Communists are altogether correct to regard Christianity as the deepest menace to their regime: the liberals in America are equally correct, from their standpoint, to urge the church to abandon its preoccupation with faith and salvation and turn, instead, to being a mentor to the all-powerful state. In the City of God there are souls who pay their taxes to Caesar willingly; who go through an entire lifetime without robbing or cheating others; who support themselves without need of the state; who give far more than they receive. The City of God, then, thrusts a dagger squarely into the politician's patronage system even while religious persons abide fully by all the law and authority of secular governors.

The Christian corollary to secular reform is faith. The secular liberal's reforming obsession is the only species of faith the nonbeliever permits himself. The Christian trusts in a transcendent and awesome and inexplicable force; a responsible and responsive Father to ease human sorrows and to comfort distress. The liberal, in a sense, is no one's son. What he does, he does bravely, without a Father, for the sake of his vision of a better world. This liberal courage is ancient and honorable but often simplistic and foolish, and often reduces to the notion that human troubles will go away if the right laws were enacted, or enough money were appropriated; or that differences of belief will be mitigated if only people will have dialogues with each other. Even so, innumerable times through modern history liberals have stood up to defend the innocent against lynchers and accusers; have stood beside the oppressed, and have assumed lonely intellectual positions in a sea of scholarly opposition. The liberal courage, vested in stubborn men who have been convinced of their own rectitude, has been phenomenal, although the decay of liberalism in recent decades has reversed the situation so that liberals now form the pack, and the occasional dissenter is a nonliberal. Frequently, in days past, liberals supplied conscience to the Christian community and spotlighted the abominations that were being done in the name of Jesus Christ. But that time is past now. Not even the civil libertarian-type liberals exercise the moral imagination that was once their hallmark.

A Christian views reform in a fundamentally different light than non-believers. The clay of the liberal potter is society, and especially the state. The clay for the Christian potter is the individual character, and especially the clay of one's own self. The object of the secular reformer is a more just and humane social structure. The object of the Christian is to expand the pool of believers on earth by increasing the number of persons who accept the governance of God and thus commit themselves to his laws, his charity, his love, and his honesty. The Christian reformer generates a new stock of virtue in the body politic; the secular reformer exploits that virtue, is informed by that virtue, and uses that pre-existing virtue to promote adjustments of law and attitude in social relationships. Ironically, the secular reformer could scarcely operate without the virtue-capital of Christianity. The liberal reformer begins by building a sort of superstructure on the great edifice of Christian belief. He begins with the observation that there are terrible injustices and cruelties in the ostensibly Christian culture. For him, Christianity is inadequate; in Jesus' doctrine there was no justice. Indeed, Jesus taught a doctrine of acquiescence in unfair worldly circumstances. He taught those in servitude not to rebel against their exploiters but to be good servants. He taught masters not to release their servants but to be good to them. He taught a doctrine of profound inequality in which those who have much would receive more while those who have little would lose what little they have. He taught a doctrine of wages and recompense that seemed totally unfair: in one parable he described a situation in which several laborers contracted for differing amounts of work at the same pay, and those who worked more than the one who did the least were envious of him. But Jesus didn't have anything to say about the alleged unfairness of it; rather, He rebuked the envy of those who had worked harder for their pay. An astonishing doctrine, and one that forces egalitarian liberals to reject Christianity as being somehow unfair, unjust, inhumane. So in the end the liberal reformers assumed the burden of improving on Christianity and very early this trend evolved into active hostility toward the orthodoxies of the faith. The absence of any egalitarian teachings, in particular, became a target of the Left. For there is nowhere in Christianity the presumption that men are equal in any worldly way. Neither in skill nor wealth nor learning nor opportunity nor

120

freedom nor comfort nor health. Nor at any point in the Gospel is there an admonition to equalize health, learning, wealth, freedom, or opportunity. On the contrary, the one theme that appears and reappears is the evil of envy—the importance of the commandment against covetousness.

For the liberal reformers whose egalitarian impulse has constructed a whole politics of envy, of redistribution, of hating and soaking the rich, this aspect of Christianity is barbarous and unbearable. For if the Christian were not terribly concerned about deep inequalities, or the opulent rich, how can the world ever be made fair? For the secular ones, what often begins as a reform of the Christian clay ends up as a rejection of the teachings of Jesus.

The politics of envy is one of the most successful in the United States and in Europe. Informed by liberal egalitarianism dating back to the French Revolution and before, there is a continual impulse to equalize extremes of wealth and misery in the modern industrial states, not through charity nor any voluntary means but through the coercions of the state. But equal opportunity is not in accord with the realities of the world and not even a totalitarian state can enforce anything like an equal crack at life for all its citizens, or guarantee an equality of health and happiness. We are too different. The circumstances into which we are born vary too broadly. Things such as geography, climate, religion, parental attitudes, quality of local schools, disease, sheer misfortune such as being orphaned, all play a role. There are poor who are happy and rich who are miserable. There are angels in slums and devils in suburbs. There are some who thrive on adversity, growing in personal strength with each calamity, but there are others who simply fold up, even though they have every opportunity. To introduce a doctrine of egalitarianism into a world so diverse is unrealistic and in the end the natural divisions reassert themselves and the world sorts out into poverty, opulence, comfort, pain, happiness, and sorrow. So far, no statist methods to repress the strong and strengthen the weak have ever succeeded. Generations of progressive income taxation, for example, have not equalized wealth in the country, but have only made it more difficult for the poor to launch their own enterprises. After half a century of alleged Communist classless society, there remains a privileged master class and only the equality of misery for the rest.

While there is no way the theoretical formula of material equality for all can be implemented by the state, Christian belief does much of the job voluntarily and without any coercion at all. For two millennia rich men have surrendered massive wealth to aid the poor, in the name of God. That is something that no modern welfare state has accomplished, nor can any state ever do what Christianity has done in aiding the poor and in equaliz-

121

ing the wealth. Under progressive government it is necessary to confiscate the wealth of the most enterprising, intelligent, and courageous to help equalize conditions, but under Christian belief no man is penalized for enterprise; rather, he is rewarded for sharing what he gained. By the same token, the progressive state subsidizes and rewards the slothful and foolish of its citizens even to the point where sloth becomes its own reward. But the gift of Christian charity is one that invokes gratitude in the recipient.

It is well to remember that reforms based on redistributing wealth —such as the social security or poverty programs—do not create new wealth. It also bears remembering that the national rise to affluence in the postwar decades has not been the result of redistribution, but the result of bold enterprise in the context of a free market. Government had precious little to do with it, and if anything may have impeded the proliferation of affluence by placing its heaviest tax burden on the middle and lower middle classes.

There are other fundamental differences between an orthodox Christian and a secular reformer. Both abhor suffering but they differ as to what should be done about it. The categories of human torment are endless: disease, physical pain, plainness of feature, melancholia, loss of loved ones, loneliness, starvation, brutality, torture, perversion, blindness, deafness, ignorance, madness, loss of limbs and organs, sheer bad luck, being orphaned. The secular man, if he were at all sensitive, wants to abolish suffering and proposes that there be good schools, hospitals, orphanages, psychiatric care, and medicine available to all through the state. But even while his reforming impulse does provide a modicum of comfort to the distressed, the sum total of human suffering does not seem to diminish. Indeed, there seems to be broad areas which the state cannot penetrate: portions of the soul that only religion can reach. There is, moreover, the suffering of those who are not social problems and who, therefore, never come to the attention of the busybody state. A middle-class woman can suffer just as deeply from widowhood as a welfare woman can, and there is nothing the government can do about it. The rich know physical pain as truly as do the poor, and the rich are capable of madness, of a deviled spirit, just as surely as the poor. Thus, when confronted with the depth and variety of human misery, the secular reformer must concede at last to his own impotence and the impotence of his engine of mercy, the coercive state. And if he tries to increase the potency of his engine of mercy by radicalizing the process, he turns the state into an authoritarian regime on the one hand, and destroys the entrepreneurial impulse of the most fruitful on the other. There is no engine of mercy more terrible than the one organized by Lenin and Stalin. So merciful is it that even now it crushes the spirit of everyone who receives its benevolences, and compels its beneficiaries to live a life of gnawing spiritual loneliness because the beneficiary next door might be an agent of those who promulgate the state's charities and mercies.

For a Christian, however, human suffering assumes a different and much more optimistic character. For one thing, because a Christian deals with the clay of personality rather than the social clay, the Christian can reach out to the private suffering of every human being, where the state can only hope to juggle the general social structure to aid the poor. The Christian approach is both to ameliorate suffering and to help its communicants triumph over their personal troubles and become stronger persons. Suffering is meaningless and inane to the secular man, and why any human should undergo misery is something the secular man can't comprehend. The Christian is more sensitive to the spiritual advancement that a person can achieve by overcoming his suffering and torment. For joy is not the fruit of an unchallenged life, but the fruit of triumph over all adversity. The man who has overcome his suffering is stronger and more generous than one who has scarcely suffered at all. The happy man is not one from whom all suffering has been removed, but one who has evolved the strength and inner peace to cope, day by day, with anything Dame Fortune tosses his way. To remove all challenge from his life is to destroy all meaning in his life. This is not to argue that suffering is good, but rather that it can be used to grow. Without it, life becomes one-dimensional, boring, and shallow. So bored has the present generation of affluent Americans become that they seek danger and challenge in their sports and games and travels. There is a search for something over which to triumph. Faith, for the Christian, is without much meaning unless it is challenged by suffering. For if there were no dilemma confronting a Christian, what would be the purpose of an abiding trust in God and His mercies? "Lead us not into temptation," Christians pray each day, asking God not to cause them to suffer more than they can endure it. St. Paul wrote in Hebrews that one should

> despise not the chastening of the Lord, nor faint when thou art rebuked of Him: for whom the Lord loveth He chasteneth and scourgeth every son whom He receiveth. If ye endure chastening, God dealeth with you as sons; for what son is he whom the father chasteneth not? . . . Now no chastening for the present seemeth to be joyous, but grievous: nevertheless, afterward it yieldeth the peaceable fruit of righteousness unto them which are exercised thereby.

123

This, then, is the meaning of suffering to Christians. It is not hardness of heart that causes them to look askance at some social reforms alleged to alleviate suffering, but rather the knowledge that suffering is terribly personal and involves personal struggle to triumph over grief. Nonetheless there is nothing clearer through the New Testament than the command to be merciful and charitable: that is, to ameliorate suffering as far as possible, and to offer love, hope, faith to those in need. But this, surely, is substantively different from the secular efforts to abolish suffering—and the life challenge of suffering—by social means.

The reformers have gone to drastic lengths, especially when dealing with children, to remove all potential suffering situations, all challenges, and most disciplines. There is a vogue among educators to eliminate competition in the classroom because the losers are supposedly wounded by their failures, and grow discouraged. This leads to grade schools without grades, without failure or the threat of failure, without praise or privileges—and ultimately without love, for no parent or teacher who truly loves a child would conceivably insulate and sterilize him from the realities of life. The net effect has been to generate young innocents so palpably weak that they collapse, cop out, when thrust into the adult world. That is what the kid cult kids do when confronted with the harshness of the world after high school. It is no wonder they don't trust adults: for all their young lives they have been closeted from anything resembling a challenge, or suffering, or learning to surmount their own inadequacies. The shock of recognition is too much. The world, even our humane, tolerant, American world, becomes a can of worms, and terrorizes the weaklings and the warped. The kids were betrayed not by generalized permissiveness but by adult protectiveness. The kids were betrayed not because they were allowed to do anything they pleased, but because they were forbidden to taste the bitterness of life or face the challenges and hurts that inevitably build true maturity. The kids were betrayed by parents who were determined to protect them from the Great Depression ordeals and all the hardships of sojourns through poverty and war. The kids know, somehow, that they have been overly pampered and that is why they cry "freedom" even amidst an incredibly free society. Some deep impulse in them hungers for the liberty to grow up. The generation gap extends not only between youths and their parents but also between youths and the state as well. The young people behave toward the state quite similarly to their behavior toward their parents. There are continual thrusting and testing to determine the limits of acceptable conduct. They complain of state repression, despite what the realities are. They project a sense of rebellion; a feeling of youthful innocence betrayed by a corrupt adult world; and not a little anger at being

124

so socialized that the harsh realities of maturity are too much with which to cope. The kids are not radicalized by an unbearable past but rather by an unbearable future. Their pasts have normally been devoid of great anguish, starvation, or misery. But their future is horrifying because they are so naked, so unequipped with strong character to cope with life's bittersweets. Their impotence is what radicalizes them: not even a quiet life in the harness of a secure job, rearing a family, seems within their capability. They know themselves to be so unstable and frightened that a routine coping capacity is beyond what they can demand of themselves. So many of them were "good, quiet children" who were rarely confronted with challenge all their young lives. The crazy kids are the fruits of a generation of reformers who never understood the challenge building blocks of character. The helter-skelter flight of the kids from real life in the vicious harbors of drugs and hip culture is the fruit of the reformers.

There exists now a generation of young Americans who are terrified to live and terrified to die, and what the consequences of their widespread weakness will be is hard to determine. They are conditioned not to regard their tribulations as innately personal; something that yields to grit, courage, sacrifice, or discipline. Rather, their conditioning compels them to believe their personal happiness rests in public measures—more eventual reforms—that will, somehow, soften an intractable world. An idea almost totally absent from any of the kid cult manifestoes, even the best of them, is one of personal rectitude as the key to a fruitful life. That is the one, unbearable, devil-idea that glows as wolf-eyes in the darkness beyond their campfires. Any collective reform is acceptable. Communes in New Mexico where they all lean on one another; big-city buying communes; big family communes; city soviets; any reform that is labeled "the people" rather than "me." These young reformers and dropouts (the two types are virtually identical) cannot bear to look inward to the mirrors of the heart. This is, to a lesser extent, true of secular liberal reformers as well, whose obsession with social manipulation masks their flight from self-development. Few, even among Christians, have learned to turn and face themselves and learn the full potential of their weakness, evil, strength, and virtue.

The courage to face the self is not something anyone can possess; it is the gift of God, given to the most fortunate on earth. And one definition of it is Grace. There is no way to reform the self without smashing the older cup; without humbling one's self before God and crying "mea culpa" for all the stored up folly and conceit and cruelty and selfishness of a lifetime, even a very young lifetime. The old cup must be smashed if the soul were to reside in a new and better vessel. What makes the smashing bearable is

125

the awakening knowledge of Divine love that penetrates even to the worst and most selfish of men. The kids who have no God, and the liberals who have no God either, can never experience the event of self-purification and forgiveness which is the prelude to a life of personal achievement. It is an event flooded with fears and almost unbearable shame; it is catharsis, and the lighting of a clear blue flame that burns away the impurities of the heart. The experience has been described many times by believers, but those who cannot bear the idea, scorn it, and scorn God.

The secular reformer can establish his humanitarianism on a wholly hypocritical basis: at the same time, he calls for grandiose reforms without the slightest sacrifice on his own part; not a dime's worth of money or an hour's worth of labor, or a moment's worth of socializing with those whose cause he trumpets. He can divorce himself totally if he wishes from his own humane program. He proposes the deployment of tax revenues—other people's money—for the target group. A Christian cannot proceed in that manner. His first concern is in the condition of that soul and body he calls his own. He cannot reform without immersing himself in the reform. Many do, of course, but they are behaving at a level something less than their aspirations. The Christian's clay is his private person: all the unruly passions and untractable habits that trouble him are his target, and the triumph over self is the reform he carries out into the world.

11. THE LOYALISTS

THE most neglected group in America is the Middle American youths who still pin their hopes on a just and free Republic. The media scorn them; the politicians studiously ignore them except as potentially milkable taxpayers who will help finance the grandiose welfare cathedrals. These are the quiet ones, the suffering, complacent, honorable people who keep the ship of state afloat.

They are preparing to enter and use the free economy. Their goals are modest: a rising affluence, security, freedom to advance, and a government that mostly keeps out of the way and has muscle enough to preserve domestic tranquility and protect them from foreign predators. They stick to their studies through college; often are less bright than the brilliant radicals. But they are made of sterner stuff than the swingers and street people who lack the perseverance to get their degrees and enter the business world.

Although they comprise a majority, they are not in the left-swinging political mainstream. Ideology is not their meat. They have inherited a practical bent for dealing with palpable problems in their careers. Some are devout; many adhere at least to the forms and norms of religion, or profess a pantheistic if not a personal God. They are centrists, wary of right-wing economic libertarianism as well as the top-heavy, tax-heavy leftist welfare state. They make good soldiers, fight loyally, and acquiesce in the draft without deep resentment because they feel a moral obligation to serve their Republic regardless of whether the service is in a good or dubious cause, and because they see their stint in the service as laden with opportunity.

The hip kids do better at establishing some community among themselves. Being radical, being alienated, being drugged and doped and engaged in assembly-line sex demolish verbal barriers, and so they talk among themselves—candidly, fluently, nakedly. And in their flooding words they find some sort of bonds and camaraderie in a lonely and bondless world.

But the square ones suffer their loneliness unalloyed. It is one of the tragedies of America that conversation is loaded with so many taboos. Those poor, straight, square kids have to avoid emotions; they must never cry. They must talk only about straight, square things, such as cars and hobbies and (ironically) sex. They must never lose face; they can never reveal their inner torments and doubts. Their social life is adapted to the standup cocktail party, where strangers come, and strangers leave. It is taboo for them to express shame, or grief, or even great joy, or public affection for each other. The straight, Middle American kids are corseted early by their corseted parents; and few critics of our society understand the corseting of Americans, or comment about it. If the squares are a silent majority, such silence exists because this nation has so many conversational taboos.

The straight kids expect more from America than do the hip kids. The alienated ones believe the country is in the hands of a few oligarchs, and opportunity is lost. But the squares still entertain some notion of progress based on their own skills, training, and wisdom. They are in this sense traditional Americans; they believe that if opportunity is there, they can take advantage of it. They believe managers are not blind, and will spot and reward talent and balanced judgment is almost any field of endeavor.

In many ways these young people will be cruelly disillusioned. The ones who have placed their faith most heavily in free capitalist enterprise are likely to be the most wounded by it when they discover the extent of politics and corruption threading through it. By and large, managements rarely reward individual enterprise and prefer to deal with large collectives, such as trade unions, for lockstep wage settlements rather than with individuals of varying skills and dedication. The loyalists will discover that the benevolent state takes an intense interest in any unusually ambitious person, not because it wishes to encourage ambition, but because it wishes to milk it. The tax structure rests most heavily on those who work the hardest and are the most progressive.

The corporations themselves are collectivist and ultrademocratic and have lost their capacity to pile rewards on their most fruitful employees. Between collectivist government and democratic business, the poor, straight young worker is bled, milked, and stomped in behalf of the others who advance by politics, agitation, and extracting tax dollars. This is the deeply discouraging reality faced by the silent squares: they ask themselves how they can advance if enterprise is no longer rewarded; corporations prefer to deal with masses of men rather than individuals; honest industry is the mark of a sucker; and brilliance is the object of venomous envy. The progressive income tax functions with special vindictiveness against the rising young, and the middle class. Congress long ago provided tax advantages for the rich, not because the rich are powerful, or because Congress loves them, or because Congress is corrupt, but rather because of the social utility of amassing capital for new jobs, for low-interest municipal bonds, for large-scale charity, or a hundred other sound reasons of state policy and wise economic management. And so, in the end, the rising, silent conformists catch the wallop of the taxes, and they hurt. Innumerable young couples survive by such expedients as moonlighting, wives working, or part-time hobby jobs. Roughly, a third of their income ultimately is absorbed by federal, state, and local taxing bodies. They are slaves a third of the year. They bear all this uncomplainingly but, nonetheless, wonder where it will all stop, especially with leftists demanding a larger and larger public sector, financed by still more levies on private incomes—and private freedom. At what point does the shrinking tax base of private business simply succumb to the parasitic bureaucracy, which may be productive in achieving social goals—such as education—but surely unproductive as a taxable resource? They wonder, further, whether some of the more pressing needs of society, such as more welfare money, might actually decline if taxes were lowered rather than raised, with the intent to create jobs, and put more spending money in people's pockets.

The Middle Americans range from plodders to geniuses, but none of them share the intoxicating voguishness of the New Left and its minions. There is a certain heady quality of belonging, of in-ness, of riding the very crest of the wave of the future, that permeates the left-radicalism: it is exhilarating and joyous, and a fertile compensation for all the other grievances and frustrations of being a hip radical. That lovely radical elitism is, usually, beyond the ken of the sober, straight kids, whose voice in politics is moderate and, therefore, unheard; quiet and, therefore, ignored.

On campuses these middle Americans find their education jeopardized by the uproars of the left and the acquiescence of faculties and adminis-

129

trators to the mayhem of the left. Their career prospects are interrupted by campus closures; the quality of their education is diminished by activist instructors, strikes, swinging professors, and street people. Some of the square ones simply have pulled up stakes and sought one of the few remaining tranquil colleges. Others have resorted to desperado tactics, such as suing radicals for disrupting education and administrators for failing to deliver the schooling they are contractually obliged to supply.

The Middle American kids are facing a sort of corruption of America that is rarely discussed or understood: the corruption of separating reward from industry and achievement. It is no longer the case that those of the finest character, those who are industrious, persevering, and wise, reap the harvest. Nor is it true any longer that the indolent, immature, and corrupt stay at the lower levels of society. They have discovered the ladder of politics to climb to positions formerly reserved to the most industrious. There is a moral and ethical disturbance that could prove ruinous to the Republic, more so than any problem dreamed up by the liberal left.

It is not a deliberate inteant of liberalism to foster this situation; indeed, liberals ideally do not wish to dampen the entrepreneurial spirit, but rather help the helpless and place a secure floor under the mass of less competent men. Such programs as social security, which consume over 10 percent of a working man's income when the employer's contribution is included, are designed with the best intentions to underwrite everyone's old age. But the effect is to sap the earning power of the young most of all; to extract income precisely when it is needed most by a newlywed couple. It forces them into a perpetual wage-earning career pattern and prohibits the sort of investments that lifted previous generations out of poverty.

The young aren't dumb. The inadequacy of bureaucratic public welfarism is blatant to them. Even though most conservative criticism of the welfare state is pointedly ignored by the media, enough breaks through at least to alert the squares, and sometimes even the alienated kids, that much is rotten and foolish on the left. Sometimes, a whole bureaucratic program, such as urban renewal, is devastated by a single book, such as Martin Anderson's *The Federal Bulldozer* which argued trenchantly that renewal simply demolished the homes, the neighborhoods, and the cheap rents of the poor while replacing the lost housing with a handful of relatively high-priced units.

But most of the square kids understand that bureaus are not profit-oriented; have a built-in growth factor; tend to achieve less and less as they balloon more and more; and are scarcely the engines of utopia. To continue to vest more power in them is to move toward tyranny by degrees.

For the straight Middle American, self-conquest is a lifelong process

130

with uncertain results and the sad promise of a lot of stumbling and retreating. The farther he goes, the more weaknesses he unearths in himself. He is inspired by some vision of what he wishes to be—usually a Christian one, although he may pattern himself on a powerful model, or on a Nietzschean superman idea. Each day offers a whole new series of problems: he learns to check his irritability toward someone. He learns to do his schoolwork early, without procrastination. He remembers someone in need, and makes sure the needy one receives some kindness. He catches himself in a fib, and remembers not to lie. He struggles to transcend his lusts and hungers, even though he often falters and the whole business of restraint sometimes seems absurd and pointless. He shakes himself out of bed Sunday mornings for church. He tackles his habitual problems, such as tardiness. He assesses himself periodically and is not afraid to make an agonizing self-appraisal. And bit by bit, as the habit of evolutionary character evolves in him, he begins to discover an inner peace and satisfaction. He is not so much at war, not so much ravaged by his hungers. He discovers that the more he uses his will, the greater is his will and ironically, the greater is his liberty. He has little patience with the undisciplined, hip kids who whine that they have no freedom; in tolerant America, a free man is one who makes himself free by the disciplining of his will and spirit. If he is a Christian, he soon discovers that for his stumbling, there are always help, comfort, and forgiveness waiting for him.

C.S. Lewis described the process this way:

> People often think of Christian morality as a kind of bargain in which God says, "If you keep a lot of rules I'll reward you, and if you don't I'll do the other thing." I do not think that is the best way of looking at it. I would much rather say that every time you make a choice you are turning the central part of you, the part of you that chooses, into something a little different from what it was before. And taking your life as a whole, with all your innumerable choices, all your life you are slowly turning this central thing either into a heavenly creature or a hellish creature: either into a creature that is in harmony with God, and with other creatures, and with itself, or else into one that is in a state of war and hatred with God, and with its fellow creatures and with itself. To be the one kind of creature is heaven: that is, joy and peace and knowledge and power. To be the other means madness, horror, idiocy, rage, impotence, and eternal loneliness.

Lewis is describing a Christian dynamism operating on those who make wrong or right decisions, and triumph over, or succumb to, their unbridled impulses. There is nothing in that dynamism that necessarily involves the state or the collectivity. Men reach sublime levels of selfhood regularly as the fruit of their own self-training rather than as the result of juggling our social institutions until they are just so. This suggests that a Christian has an attitude that is frightful heresy to liberals and the left: it is that the nature of our social institutions is not terribly important unless they are violently tyrannical or dangerously lax. Men can and do achieve inward strength, strong will, and high virtue under American capitalism and the open society; in socialist England; in Franco's Spain; under Latin military juntas; in the claptrap African ministates, and even in the less drastic Yugoslavian and Polish Communist régimes. But in the Soviet Union and Red China, or in ultrapermissive Denmark or Sweden, the task is immeasurably more difficult.

The square citizen has within him the knowledge of salvation that has no relevance to the state, or "society." His potters clay is his own self and not the society that absorbs the reformers. Indeed, the square rightfully suspects that reformers are cop-outs; ones who abandon the more exacting, honorable, difficult and rewarding task of turning themselves into highly individualized strong-charactered, self-sufficient men and women. Hence, the abiding scorn toward the do-gooders that one uncovers among the squares. It isn't that anyone objects to doing good or is complaining about the multifarious efforts to alleviate the world's endless suffering, but rather that so many such reformers are cop-outs who cannot muster the courage to help themselves. They try to reform the world, instead, with predictable impracticality and danger to free institutions.

Collectivists are appalled by the nonchalance of the run of men toward reform. They call it apathy, or reaction, or callousness, or hatred, because they do not see the "apathetic" and "callous" quietly struggling with inward devils, or helping neighbors instead of the welfare state, or quietly serving as stewards in their churches; or most significantly of all, disciplining themselves to be fruitful for a lifetime so they need not be a burden on others. The squares are preoccupied with setting aside a retirement income; insuring themselves against calamity; putting kids through college without the help of the welfare state. The strong, healthy, dull squares are the virtuous citizens whom collectivists at once resent and exploit. (Resent because the strong don't need the welfare state; exploit because they are the only steady source of surplus capital and private stability.) Freedom itself, in most western nations, is overwhelmingly a matter of the individual's triumph over his environment rather than a matter of public balances and structures.

132

The squares, then, are the heretics in the context of the secular social gospel. They can and do function admirably without a by-your-leave from the collectivist left. The ultimate insult liberalism suffers is the dark knowledge that the workaday world could function admirably if there were not a liberal in sight with all his social blueprints; worse, that there would be no more miscarriage of justice without liberals around than with them on hand in swarms; and, quite probably, more freedom than exists under the most liberal regimes.

It is even worse a heresy to suggest that the average Middle American is more libertarian that the liberals. It is true that the liberal mentality is zealous in its defense of certain freedoms, especially those involving speech, thought, and conscience, as well as political gathering, petitioning, and organizing. In these areas liberals are fanatic and dogmatic libertarians. As defenders of academic freedom, liberals are actually militant. And in the realms of private morality, liberals are obsessive libertarians and resent even the mildest invasions of the state.

But because politics and language arts bulk so importantly in liberal eschatology, there is a presumption among them that free speech and related freedoms are all that matter. How wrong! The straight people in all walks of life, the professions, the unions, the offices and assembly lines, the mines and farms, and on the ships at sea, know that the liberty to speak freely is only a relatively small, albeit important, corner of the sum total of human liberty. The most important freedom—the one truly separating us from totalitarian nations— is economic. To the extent we are free to pursue the livelihood of our choice, in a free labor and price market, to negotiate our own pay; to invest and save our capital; to escape confiscatory taxes; to own and control property; to function in business with a minimum of state regulation— to be free to do all these things and enjoy all these liberties, is to be free in a way the liberal left will not tolerate or even contemplate. Whole societies can function relatively freely without free speech, for example, Spain and South Africa. But no man is free in the Soviet Union either to speak his mind or to become an entrepreneur; to make money, to achieve comfort and safety. Liberal criticism of the Soviets is generally directed only toward its suppression of free speech. Liberals are notoriously silent about communism's heavy oppression of the more meaningful economic liberties. It is obvious that a man who builds a business and achieves independent means is less and less dependent on the state. He is mobile and free, and his very economic strength, in league with countless other business and professional citizens, check-reins the grasping and greedy politicians. All this is patently clear to those Middle American citizens whose major sin, in liberal eyes, is to retain a dour

133

suspicion of all politicians. A sense of liberty is more deeply vested in the phlegmatic squares, those benighted Babbitts, than in the sporty liberals whose programs invariably, decade after decade, shrink the sum of options for most men—except in that narrow, exotic corner of free speech and expression. So statist have liberals become, in fact, that they lost the semantic advantage of a name associated with liberty: the proper term now for those who still advocate the broad spectrum of economic and social laissez faire is libertarian, rather than liberal.

Free speech bulks so large among academics, newsmen, lawyers, and politicians, who use speech as their tool of livelihood, that it is difficult for them even to comprehend how unimportant it is to the Middle Americans who need other freedoms, such as a free marketplace, to survive. In truth, a square citizen does not feel one whit abused by antisedition laws, or laws outlawing pornography, or laws against conspiracy, or laws separating political assembly from political mayhem—or any of the laws most liberals find repressive, archaic, and unreasonable. Such laws seem reasonable to square people because they are simply not interested in fostering sedition, or mayhem, or anarchy, or pornography and, indeed, regard such things as threats to the good society. They believe such laws are ultimately designed to defend the liberties and tranquilities of the people and to aid the state in resisting the activities of every two-bit totalitarian. There is a notion on the left that totalitarianism rises only when the freedom to speak freely is curtailed: actually, it begins when the state institutes draconian economic measures, usually well in advance of any curtailment of speech. Indeed, the loss of economic freedom normally precedes the loss of political and verbal freedoms. That is to say, a country may be communized thoroughly and the major liberties dead before its liberals even begin to feel the noose around their freedom of expression.

None of this, of course, is to denigrate the value of free speech or the need for free assembly and free politics. There is good in liberals' vigilance in behalf of this corner of human liberty. Our radical minorities, from Black Panthers to John Birchers, can largely thank a vigilant liberalism for ensuring the freedom to assert things that go against the public grain. There is some question whether liberals actually practice free speech for others with the same zeal they reserve to themselves; but that is another matter.

On the other hand, the Babbitts generally fall short of defending the economic freedoms they profess. Their adherence to free market capitalism weakens noticeably when their business is threatened by cheap foreign imports or sharp domestic competition. Their homage to the most

134

efficent producers withers substantially when the best competitors turn out to be other than themselves, or happen to be Japanese or West German. At that point the free-trading Babbitts become sudden proponents of high tariffs, protected markets, taxes on the other guys, quotas, tax breaks, or other subsidies for themselves, and general autarky in economics (the notion that a country should produce all the goods it needs within its borders so as not to be dependent on foreign trade, regardless of who or what can produce any goods most cheaply). So ambiguous is Middle America's adherence to capitalism that, ironically, the system suffers less from liberal interventions than from the "fence-me-in" legislation proposed by the squares. It is possible—nay, probable—that American business could unwittingly demolish free enterprise simply by continuing to pressure government for tariffs, quotas, regulated prices on both labor and goods, more licensing, and more regulated monopoly. The free enterprisers have reached the point of begging for subsidies rather than letting the losers go out of business—which is a way of perpetuating incompetence. By all rights if a Lockheed Corporation fails to remain solvent, it should expire rather than beg the government for aid. If Penn Central can't make it, it should be dismantled and sold to whatever groups—other railroads and trucklines—that can provide the service at a profit.

Middle Americans are deeply skeptical of reform, perhaps because they understand that each change in law produces effects utterly unanticipated by even the most informed and sagacious legislators. Quite accidentally, reforms stomp out some businesses and create new ones. Few in New York State, for example, envisioned that the state's liberal abortion reform would generate a horde of abortion hucksters and brokers who, for a fat fee, steered the damsels to the abortion mills. Private skepticism runs deeper even than questioning the efficacy of reform. It runs to a wholly different outlook on life; an outlook that holds that a man's private character is the best guarantee of his happiness and the happiness of others. The private citizen rightly suspects that if the left could suddenly initiate every single reform in its manifesto; that is, if the liberal left suddenly had carte blanche to rebuild America as it sees fit—that the Leftists would not find their cravings assuaged nor would they be happier, nor comforted, nor would the freaks be healed and the minorities lifted from misery. The private man is skeptical precisely because he perceives a natural limit on what public reform can achieve—a limit that is not perceived by radicals and liberals. A private man believes that personal viciousness will not wither away by manipulating the state or rebuilding the environment, not even the school environment, nor even by applying the insights of psychia-

135

try. The private man perceives something in the nature of original sin—intractable evil, or imperfection—that cannot be wiped out by science, or government, or even George Gallup. Surely the clay of man is unchanged under communism, where the state has ultimate power and no facet of Soviet society escapes the whim of its masters. There are thefts, black markets, lies, and cynicism among Soviet citizens. There has been no decline of cruelty, lust, wickedness. No abandonment of divorce, no decline of adultery. No waning of fear and hatred. If anything, the people are more brutal, perverse, and cowering than the ones who peopled the novels of Tolstoy or Dostoevski.

But, of course, the left argues that the liberal state will be democratically governed—that the rascals can be thrown out even if they have great economic and social power. But whether or not the old rascals can be exchanged for new rascals bears little on the question of whether the state is the natural engine of utopia; whether the state can substitute for what the Christian calls the Comforter, the Holy Spirit described in Acts, who comes into the hurt, the lonely, the distressed, and sorrowful, with a healing mercy and comforting love.

Increasingly, the Middle Americans find themselves being labeled fascists or nazis by those of the radical left. The term is puzzling because it is so inappropriate; so much a product of a twisted teleology. For those who fought against fascists and Nazis in World War II, the idea is preposterous. The mislabeling emerges from a generation that has had no contact with those ideologies and whose knowledge of the twin ideologies of the axis powers is limited to histories written by liberal historians. On the American political spectrum, both nazism and fascism are properly grouped on the left, that is, on the side of expanded government, deep intervention in the economy, socialism, and public solutions to conflicts that may have roots in private life. The effort to group these collectivist ideologies with the older American tradition of severely limited government, individualism, and private enterprise, is simply absurd and ignorant. American political tradition prior to the New Deal had a deep republican—even anarchist—quality: a genuine federalism that dispersed rather than centralized power; a constitution that severely limited executive authority and federal power; low taxes; minimal state control of business. How bizarre, then, to group the adherents of limited, decentralized government and free enterprise with the adherents of a system of state socialism in which free competition was abolished, wages and prices were controlled, unions were run by the state, power was centralized into a single dictator and ruling party; a massive welfare state with relief,

136

medical care, job security, recreation programs, and a host of other tax-paid benefits was imposed on everyone; and in which the military was the natural adjunct of the welfare state (as has been the case here since the New Deal!). How bizarre to group centripetal fascism with centrifugal republicanism! Both fascists and liberals adopted Keynesian economic nostrums involving state monetary manipulation. Both created welfare states. Both enormously expanded military machines. Both smashed constitutional barriers against big government and vested enormous—even totalist—powers in the chief executive.

When the Middle American is called a fascist, therefore, he is presumed by the kid cults to believe in things he finds abominable. If "fascist" and "nazi" are the key pejorative terms of our times, then those who casually hurl them cannot help but be splattered by their own mud. It was the Nazis who evolved and used street politics, marches, invasions of legislative chambers, fires and bombings, and defiance of constituted authority. They were soulmates of today's Weathermen, and shared an ideology which—except for its racism and Jew-baiting—is in accord with modern liberalism, especially in the broad sphere of economics. John Kenneth Galbraith's prescriptions for deepening federal operation of the economy are a neat compendium of fascist and nazi nostrums.

The two main links allegedly linking Middle Americans to the fascists are racism and militarism. But even these are tenuous. Most squares do support the flag in combat—but usually hate war and mobilize into civilian armies only with deep reluctance. Republican America has always been too busy with its frontiers and commerce to be militarist. Support for committed troops is one thing; an obsession with the military itself à la European fascism—is quite another. Few of America's squares are militarists; few have organized into paramilitary groups such as the Hitler Youth. Few are eager to serve in the army. The graying veterans of World War II are mostly conscripts who regarded the military not with Prussian delight, but as bewildered, skeptical civilians, eternally suspicious of military stupidity and authoritarianism. Neither do many square Americans seriously support a policy of military expansion, such as was part of fascist ideology. The squares don't covet Canada or Mexico or Latin America. If they approve of the deployment of American troops abroad, it is to help America's friends resist modern totalitarianism rather than to plant the American flag on foreign soil.

Much of America is, in a sense, racist. In the South the blacks are still consciously segregated and persecuted; in the North they are simply ignored and ghettoized. But this scarcely demonstrates the existence of fascism in America. Italian fascism wasn't even racist until Hitler began imposing his anti-Semitic ideas on the cosmopolitan, urbane Italians. Even then, the Italians went about it in such a half-hearted way that racism or ethnicity was never a serious factor in Italian fascism. Racism, in any case, is not a phenomenon limited to rightist ideology, although it was a major prop of the German National Socialists. Racism persists in Soviet Russia, socialist England, capitalist United States, Castro's Cuba, Red China, and most everywhere else. It simply can't be pinned exclusively to any American class nor does its existence prove that a nation is fascist or totalitarian. Most racism is a cultural suspicion of other peoples; the Nazis exploited that fear most, but not exclusively, and not in any fashion that would be tolerated in the United States. To call American Babbitts fascist because they are allegedly racist is a most tendentious and dubious exercise in logic.

The accusation that the Middle Americans are "authoritarian" is more apt, although laden with irony, and the astute conformist ought to accept the label with no loss of dignity. It is used, of course, in a pejorative sense by the left; and leftist scholars are forever producing studies purporting to show the "authoritarian personalities" in middle America as insecure and nasty people who seek to dominate others and destroy others' liberties. The portrait is a caricature. From the left's standpoint, any institution or belief that prevents anyone from doing anything is bad. Freedom is professed to be an absolute (except for businessmen) and the enemies of freedom turn out to be God, His church, all businessmen, the FBI, tradition, anything old, most of the Constitution, all rural people, all people who are not part of the academic community, all conservatives, all economic libertarians, and, of course, the military.

The list is riddled with irony. Barry Goldwater would cut taxes by half and voluntarize the armed forces—but that doesn't count. Libertarians would abolish most regulation of business—but that doesn't count. The church provides a pathway from slavery to drugs, or sex, or alcohol—but that doesn't count, either. The conservatives wish to decentralize power, bring it closer to home, foster variety among states rather than uniform federal standards—but that doesn't count either. God promises that his yoke will be easy for all believers, and they would be able to conquer their inner conflicts—but neither does that count. The FBI and military secure the freedom of virtually all citizens against foreign and domestic enemies—but that doesn't count either. So far as the obsessed left is concerned, all but itself is repressive, authoritarian, and, therefore, bad.

But the word *authoritarian* is acceptable nonetheless. It suggests the acceptance of authority. True Christians accept a revealed authority, i.e., a definite construct of moral and ethical law that must be adhered to as a duty. This law is believed to be transcendent, and thus divinely ordained: vested in the moral law is the power of God. The law is to be sanctified and venerated; it requires the searching humility of the believer. All these ideas are anathema to the left, and to secular man, who sees no moral force or authority beyond community consensus, and who supposes that morals may change as the consensus changes. The idea of a moral force that is unchanging and transcending human intelligence and passion is to his thinking the perfect proof that a large body of western men make slaves of themselves and others. Worse, the church believes in a free will; holds men accountable for all they do, even though, in the estimation of the secularists, scientists have demonstrated that man is a creature tossed and blown by the forces of the id and super-ego, and by family conditioning, and the behavioral mechanisms that make choice always an illusion. Again, we reach an irony: for what secular men are arguing is that it is slavery to have a free will and be held accountable; that man should be freed of so grave a responsibility because he is not able to control his acts. He ought not to be punished severely for transgressions nor rewarded substantially for successes because these are accidents of nature; or the result of being poor, or wealthy, etc. Freedom, by leftist definition, consists of being liberated from responsibility; especially responsibility for others; in being unpunished for what one can't help anyway.

Most secular men shy away from their own dogma on the subject and search for some vestigial authority in community consensus or one's own evolved conscience. The great vogue of "situational ethics" is an attempt by secular and left-moderates to retain some sort of controlling mechanism upon personality, that is, to impose some tenuous authority over anarchic behavior. But even it belies the more radical beliefs of the behaviorists—that all conduct is ordained by conditioning, and free will is an illusion. Situation ethics does presuppose rational choice, although it rejects transcendent moral authority. It is built, in the main, on the Golden Rule. In any given situation the criterion is whether it will damage others. Extramarital sex is considered usually undamaging, but in situation ethics adultery could be construed as a desirable thing: it might provide relief or joy and happiness to a woman with an impotent husband, for example. Although the hip kids, sometimes, go the whole route and reject all authority, their secular elders—the traditional liberals—generally blend the old moral capital of Christianity with their own permissiveness and nihilism to arrive at a flexible conscience. They can conclude that it is no great crime

139

for a poor man to steal, for example, yet still suppose something is rather wrong with theft. The Christian and Jew find the moral law much simpler: "Thous shalt not steal." The authority is unquestioned.

The Middle Americans are authoritarians because they recognize and venerate things greater than themselves. To recognize genius in other men is inherently authoritarian; it supposes that there are authoritative standards that validate genius and brilliance. One of the phenomena of the secular left is its democracy of respect: it is a debunking and reductive ideology which belittles the great; and, therefore, it is antiauthoritarian. There is, in the thinking of Middle Americans, authority vested in many things larger than self: society, the organized nation, is an object of some reverence and honor. People of great status and power are to be rendered their just due. Community opinion, right or wrong, deserves to be weighed carefully because it is generally based on the general run of man's experience. All of these values beyond the self are essentially authoritarian and he who accepts them accepts the authority of community, nation, consensus, tradition, history, wisdom, genius, and governorship.

Perhaps Middle Americans are a bit schizoid: they are willing to ride the revolutionary tiger of a free market capitalism which is the most dynamic and disruptive force in the world—infinitely more upsetting than the sedate, secure, socialist societies. At the same time, Middle Americans have a natural, pious respect for the old verities and social arrangements. They yearn for a settled society, grouped in smaller towns, informed by orthodox loving and stern religion. They yearn for established values and customs: honor to whom honor is due, respect for elders and parents; moderation in the use of liquor; the evolution of a strong, stable neighborhood and neighborliness. They have no truck with "the good old days" economically, but for the rest they oft look backward. There is a deep nostalgia in America for a Grandma Moses existence: a return to innocence, and land, and neighbors, and the beckoning pew every Sunday. That the old innocence is gone is as much the fault of racing capitalism as it is the conscious labor of the secular left. And there are other non-ideological factors, such as an exploding population, that have contributed. In particular, capitalism revolutionarized agriculture and drove the innocents to Gomorrah.

The moral and social dilemma faced by the Middle Americans who affirm free enterprise and Christianity in the same breath is the problem of the valuation of riches and material wealth. Even though there have been innumerable efforts to reconcile affluence with Christian spiritual truths, the synthesis has never been satisfactory. Either getting and spending are

140

important, or they aren't. It is well and good to note Adam Smith's invisible hand at work: one man's drive for wealth enriches others, and the commonweal. The poor benefit from the rising standards. But in truth, the inexorable rise in poverty standards has little to do with Christianity. Jesus Christ did not preach a doctrine that involved the improvement of the lot of the poor exclusively through alterations of the social or economic system. And as for affluence, the accumulation of wealth that is widely extolled as the American system, he rejected, warning that men should seek treasure in heaven, and not earthly treasure that rusts and corrupts. One cannot serve God and Mammon at the same time: there are those among the young Babbitts whose church is Free Enterprise.

One can strive for wealth, or at least comforts, for one's family. One can give sons and daughters opportunities, and a crack at the comfortable life. Well and good. But not necessarily a Christian ideal, even though relatively unselfish motives are involved. Christianity recognizes comfort of the body as a valid goal. It is not purely a spiritual religion. But the Middle Americans mix the goals until they are convinced that Christian duty and teaching underride their quest for wealth, when, at best, it tolerates money and warns that it must relegated to more important spiritual considerations. Perhaps they learned this alchemy from their elders whose respectable middle-class churches are as much a monument to affluence as to God.

The capitalist "system" is, rather, a nonsystem because it is loose, flexible, and relatively free. It is not inherently anti-Christian the way the socialist economic system is, with its explicitly anti-Christian doctrines of leveling and organized envy. Much depends on the motives of each individual within the system: under capitalism he is free to place material well-being foremost or not; free to exploit or not; free to pinch pennies or not. Market competition is a hard taskmaster, but less hard than state taskmasters in other economic structures. It is possible, indeed commonplace, for a man to be a good Christian and find advantage under capitalist economics. Indeed, some of the great business empires were erected by men whose Christian vision inspired a deeper moral obligation in trade and service than their more rapacious competitors. The capitalist system, then, has little bearing on a man's religious belief. It is neutral, something to be used with stewardship, or used with exploitation, as an individual's conscience permits. The squares, both adult and young, err in attributing to capitalism virtues it lacks, especially the "virtue" of being inherently Christian.

But if the straight ones are too quick to lump a loose-knit economic system with the teachings of Christ who taught the value of sharing, the leftists are all too quick to equate the various species of socialism to the teachings of Jesus. Socialistic doctrine is more explicitly and relentlessly materialistic than capitalism, and is built on patterns of envy and egalitarianism explicitly condemned and rejected by Jesus. There is nothing quite so grimly anti-Christian as a state organized so that each person "gets his share." Socialism wipes out Christian generosity and charity and organizes all the envious and hateful spirits of man to insure no enterprising person rises an iota above the pack. Socialism attempts to institutionalize Christian charity, but succeeds only in mocking the very virtues Jesus taught, by reducing charity to political interest-lobbying for public funds. When charity becomes a matter of taxation and coercion and politics, it is no longer charity.

There is a widespread condemnation of permissive child-rearing among Middle Americans, but the condemnation has that peculiar quality and tone of scapegoating: it is the process of slamming others for a vice practiced by themselves. Most of America's squares have unconsciously inherited and accepted a fairly rigorous system of child-management; a system that condemns "spoiling" the youth with indulgences. It condemns neglect and excessive guidance, both. It holds that discipline firmly and consistently applied by both parents is a part of love and a way of teaching the child adult boundaries and goals. And yet, the least disciplined children in America are not the progeny of secular liberals—but of affluent suburban Middle Americans. Not only have innumerable parents of this class virtually abandoned the kids to their own devices but also literally buy them off with cars, trips, and other prizes. It is this class, paying perpetual lip service to the old pieties of child-rearing, that has betrayed its own children and ripened them for a life as alienated New Leftists. A surprising number of habitués of the crash pads park their Porsches on the streets outside. There is a spiritual corruption running deep through the affluent classes; a corruption that rots the very citizens who pay homage to the old virtues: individualism, patriotism, and God. It is not merely that they don't really believe the ideas of their fathers. This is the class of cynics who consider capitalism to be organized pillage even though they profess allegiance to the capitalist system. This is the class that rejects religion in practice simply by ignoring the church and its teachings, but never quite abandons the moral aura and mantle of faith, because it is socially becoming and graceful. This is the class that populated Westchester and suburban New

142

York; much of San Francisco, and all the other fashionable places. This is the class that sends its progeny not to Yale, but to the crash pads of Haight-Ashbury, to the radical clubs and societies, where the kids express their hate of American corruption and loathe the hypocritical adherence to unpracticed norms.

12. THE CONSERVATIVES

CONSERVATISM is a large tent with innumerable strains of thought camped within. There is no "line" among most conservatives nor any hope that this or that single reform will usher in Zion. There are as many things separating the strains of conservatism as holding them together, which puzzles those outside the tent, who would reduce the movement to a unified ideology with a thrust toward a distinctive goal.

This loose congeries of viewpoints on the right breaks into two logical subgroupings: the libertarians and the traditionalists. The libertarians are essentially classical liberals who trust the state and its engines of coercion no more than did John Stuart Mill. The traditionalists are those who, wittingly or unwittingly, defend Christian values if not the faith, as well as other venerable institutions and insights that have done good service across the generations. There has been a serious effort to synthesize the two wings, especially in the writings of Frank S. Meyer and M. Stanton Evans. They argue that the libertarian impulse could not exist except when illumined by moral and ethical insights stemming from religion. In a free, libertarian society, with the state reduced to a practical minimum they argue, the religious understanding that theft and chicanery and violence are wrong, is essential to freedom. A pack of thieves requires more, not less, government. The synthesizers argue that the prerequisite to a limited libertarian state is good order; that liberty flourishes only in a climate of certitude in which malefactors are brought to heel and social tumults are repressed. The central ideology of the right, that is, favors a limited state which, nonetheless, diligently maintains public order; very little law, but law well enforced without favor; very little moral legislation, but a moral citizenry informed by an active and authoritative church; private individualism, but balanced against a deeply merciful and charitable attitude toward others.

But these sweeping generalizations are about as far as conservatives lean toward ideology. Unlike the left, where there is a discernible line on issue after issue and where powerful arbiters set the tone in certain key publications, the right has no distinct line and each conservative welds together a viewpoint that contains not only his intellectual rationalizations but also his pieties, hopes, and attitudes as well. A conservative viewpoint contains visceral attitudes and traditional belief in addition to a rational viewpoint. There are allied cults, such as Ayn Rand's Objectivism, which is a radical libertarianism with a heady condescension toward "altruism" or "mysticism" by which the cultists mean charity and religion. Ayn Rand's followers, while militant capitalists with an insight into capitalism's remarkable dynamism and benefactions, are, nevertheless, so antireligion and schematic that Whittaker Chambers, writing in *National Review*, literally ostracized them.

The conservative synthesis has not been successful even though, ironically, it is simply an intellectual reconstruction of the single viewpoint most Americans took for granted in pre-New Deal days. The idea of a limited state to insure economic opportunity and private liberty, illumined by rich traditions of church and a close-knit community life is, after all, the torchlight of the Republic and those who sought to put liberty and tradition into harness to pull the surrey were doing no more than affirming and rationalizing America's apple pie past.

However, the schism on the right has not healed, and now conservatism is sundering into two deeply opposed camps. In one sense there no longer is a single conservatism. The radical libertarians and Ayn Rand types have moved toward right-wing anarchy and are dallying in the bordello of the New Left. The anarchists ally with the left on most questions of public moral law, and generally oppose public restraints on, say, pornography or extramarital sex. Radical libertarians espouse an equally radical individualism that seeks to cast off what few remaining bonds of community exist in America. Like the liberals, they dissent for its own sake—for the sake of self and personal identity. The anarchist right is militant, a movement with the same ideological intransigence as the New Left. It will work politically and, perhaps, seditiously to reduce government drastically and

146

will not hesitate to form alliances with the left to squash such statist activity as the Vietnam war and conscription. Right-wing anarchists argue that the traditional conservatives were seduced by a phony Cold War into advocating a garrison state with a vastly more powerful government which grew out of bounds in the '50s and '60s even more than it did through the New and Fair Deals. However, this analysis does not account for the even more rapid expansion of the welfare state, which can scarcely be laid to the cold war, and which was stoutly resisted by almost all conservatives for three decades.

The traditionalists, on the other hand, inherited not only a classical libertarian distrust of big government and the benevolent superstate but also (1) a knowledge and fear of expansionary communism; (2) an understanding that Christianity, or rather Judeo-Christian tradition, is the illumining force that enlightens western man and restrains the barbarism underlying us all; (3) that the state, also illumined by the church, can and should enforce certain common moral strictures; (4) that community with its bonds of friendship and cooperation is seriously threatened by technology and other factors and ought to be restored if possible; and (5) that ancient prescription and custom are built on trial and error, contain much immanent wisdom, and deserve veneration when passed down to us by history's seamless web. Principal spokesmen for this viewpoint are Russell Kirk and William F. Buckley Jr.

The conflict between libertarians and traditionalists has tended to conceal an even deeper and more implacable schism on the right: the problem of faith. The libertarians, especially in their new radical costume, are secular men with no religious quarrel with either liberalism or the New Left. The traditionalists tend, but not so rigorously, to be religious and are generally drawn from the congregations of the faithful. There are, of course, innumerable private variations especially among those who still try to straddle the two camps. M. Stanton Evans, for example, who helped build the earlier synthesis is, in his own words, "a defrocked methodist," i.e., one who is not active in his church, but nonetheless retains a respect for religion and its good work. Libertarianism is becoming, in fact, a new code word for a secularity that rejects all supernatural belief and its transcendent authority. Libertarians accept the New Left observation that the United States is oppressive and fascist; indeed, in libertarian circles the word *fascist* is used without reservation against traditional conservatives, and fascism is somehow equated with the enforcement of Christian ethical, moral, and spiritual belief. Under the new political dispensation there are secular libertarians—the progressives of left and right—and "fascist" Christians, who adhere to the old ways,

147

the old strictures and liberties. This whole cosmology of belief is shifting into a secular camp and a religious camp, and almost unconsciously innumerable people are packing their intellectual bags and moving. The traditional conservative camp has opened to a surprising number of religious liberals who do not wish to abandon the faith of their fathers or to join the radicals on the secular left. Likewise, the secular ones on the right are decamping to the New Left: conservatism is losing a wing of its adherents. Recent conventions of Young Americans for Freedom have highlighted the schism. Libertarian guru Karl Hess, a former Goldwater speechwriter in 1964, has mounted hippie platforms to spread the new Gospel of Anarchy according to St. Ayn. The future will witness an even deeper schism on the right because Christianity is irreconcilable with any secular belief. The true radical element in the conservative stew is Jesus Christ, whose doctrine is unalloyable.

The deepening schism on the right is grounded in two irreconcilable views or attitudes about man and his destiny. Man must either be a totally free agent (the ultimate view of the secular libertarians and classical liberals) or man must accept a higher authority beyond himself (the attitude of traditionalist Christians). The left, and now right-wing libertarians, use the polemical word *authoritarian* to describe the viewpoint of those who accept a disciplining God, or the power of those in authority on earth to discipline in the name of God. And perhaps the word, for all its pejorative connotations, is not amiss. For merely to stand in the presence of God is to be aware of a goodness and omniscience and power that demand utter obedience and suggest that such obedience to the Master ought to be the normal condition of the bulk of men. But there are distinctions here that few libertarians are willing to make. There are degrees and types of authority, and one errs to suppose that he who accepts God's authority would accept, say, a fascist dictatorship or a strongman régime. The potency of authority ranges from the teaching power to the coercive total state. Tradition and veneration play their roles. Community consensus and ostracisms occupy intermediate ground on the scale of authority. God's authority is paradoxically the most mild and severe: mild because all are free to reject it; severe because it becomes a radical facet of personality in those who accept it. Mild because ''the yoke is easy'' for those who believe; severe because those who partially believe are caught in a terrible inner agony of doubt and contradiction.

But if God were a myth, as the libertarian and secular impulse suggests, then man is a fool to bind himself to revealed commandments, and, in that case, he ought to do as he will, and the state ought to keep out of his way, or at least do no more than insure that his liberties are not abridged by

148

others. One can understand a life motivated by faith and virtue—two positive and noble goals toward which to strive. But it is more difficult to conceive of a life devoted to extending freedom for its own sake. What is freedom? What is the absence of restraint? How is man made happier by striving for freedom alone as the be-all of his existence? Conservatives often have criticized liberals for their obsession with democracy, which is only a means, a mechanical approach to government, rather than an end. But couldn't the conservative-libertarian obsession with freedom be criticized on the same ground? Freedom is a means; a milieu; the end of the political order perhaps, but not the end of personal existence. As with democracy, it is a welcome and treasured circumstance that enables us to control our destinies, but in itself it is not the goal of our personal lives. Virtue is.

The libertarian whose personal goal is total freedom walks in a quicksand of trouble. For one thing, as with his liberal counterparts and those in the kid cults, he confuses his private life with the goals of the polis, with those of the political and social order. He can achieve the ultimate social laissez faire only to discover an emptiness and nihilism within himself amidst his splendid liberty. But more likely he finds a certain ironic law of wills functioning: the greater the degree of absolute liberty to individuals tolerated by society, the more deeply he finds himself hobbled and hogtied by inexplicable inner inadequacies which prevent him from exercising his vast liberty. The world becomes perverse. It is as though he alone were strait-jacketed in a world where everyone else seems to be flapping his arms. The paradox of character is that a free spirit is bred in adversity; that is, one's liberty is nurtured not by social freedom but by repeated adventitious rebukes and wounds and frustrations which have been duly and resolutely met. The human character bursts free of something: when there is no resistance or abrasion there is no evolving character. The paradox can be expressed this way: in a totally free and permissive society individuals are trapped in their own insuperable prisons of weakness. But in a society with some authority and tradition, with norms and parental discipline hammering the infantile will into an instrument of achievement and confidence, the emerging adult is able to master more and more of life's outrages, and pushes the shores of repression farther and farther back until he is, in fact, a free man. Youngsters have established "free" communes within a very free and tolerant American society. In their own cults the kids can do pretty much as they will, even to the point of avoiding a livelihood and taxes. No authority is on hand to say nay, except perhaps on the margins of violence, such as bombing episodes. But are the kids free in their culture? Does anyone in the entire Woodstock generation run with

149

his freedom to produce anything of value? Where are their Beethovens, Bachs, Michelangelos, Edisons, Shakespeares, and Disraelis? But it may be argued that the kids use their freedom not to achieve; not to be pushed into the genius-race, not to develop strong character. Then the question becomes: What is their vaunted freedom for? To waste a life in carnality and indulgence? Is that the end of their existence and the purpose of their alien cults within the American culture? Is it to be different and adopt a mode of dress and behavior at odds with traditional people? If so, they are not free but tied negatively to fashion and tradition just as surely as conformists conform. The rubbish heaps of humanity are filled with two types: those who have been so oppressed by serfdom that their lives have sunk into stupidity and inertia; and those who have been so profoundly free and nihilistic that they become vegetables, helpless before adversity. The cry for more freedom—especially in a free and tolerant milieu—masks the cry of the impotent who really hunger for a modicum of mastery over self so that they can begin to master their environment. Those who bleat the loudest for liberty just now are somehow the ones most helpless, the ones who go to pieces when a gadget falters, or a friend rebukes, or they are rebuffed by employers and civil magistrates. The ones who cry for liberty are the ones most easily gulled by peddlers of junk and get-rich-quick artists. The obsessed libertarians are the ones who wonder to what degree they are mature men and women able to cope. The weak build their own jails for security, and their cry for freedom does not reflect a deeper hunger for boundaries. Who is less free than an obsessed libertarian? One can spot his brand of freedom by its oppressiveness.

The traditionalist-conservative cherishes liberty, as does the libertarian, but places it in a certain perspective. Libertarians have discovered a corollary between the amount of freedom existing in a society and the output of genius and productivity from that society. Their formula is simple: free men from all restraint and there will be a breathtaking upward leap in fruitfulness, progress, genius, and virtue, as men learn to govern themselves. The libertarians—and classical liberals and individualists—often cite nineteenth-century England as the freest society, and the incubator of much of the world's genius. It is true that England of that and other centuries produced an extraordinary flowering of brilliance and progress. But can all this be laid to a climate of unusual economic and social freedom? Nineteenth-century England was the era of Queen Victoria and a moral code so rigorous that it would chafe even the most conservative moderns. It was a period when vestiges of serfdom remained; the aristocracy was still potent, suffrage limited, and the church chained the nation to a distinct orthodoxy. Even the vaunted economic freedom of the era was impinged at all points by state interventions and charters, taxes, and royal manipulations to take the Union Jack wherever traders went. A traditionalist-conservative would point to deep community, homogeneity, and cohesion in England of the past century. Britons were not free in the modern libertarian sense of the term: they were everywhere hemmed in by social values so strong that they stamped the national character and made the Englishman a distinct breed recognizable anywhere in the world. The traditionalist might suggest that genius and intellectual progress seem to occur most readily when pushing against some resisting force, rather than in a climate of pure laissez faire. John Stuart Mill, for instance, struggled against a variety of communal beliefs in his essay on liberty. He could not have written that essay today in modern America. Darwin, another of England's nineteenth-century geniuses, pushed against what he conceived to be erroneous accounts of the creation and against a primitive conception of biology that involved little more than pigeonholing. The point is that genius is not produced by abandoning restraint alone, but by building on the past and balancing freedom against the claims of good authority.

We have witnessed for two centuries a liberal individualism that has scorned the restraints of community and custom in favor of the untrammeled evolution of self. This is the root of the great dread of conformity existing in the educated classes today. The early liberal individualism sought a climate of freedom in which each person could flower; indeed, even now that idea illumines much of our thinking on both the left and right. For generations this thrust toward free individuality has been incredibly fruitful. It produced in America a race of entrepreneurs that tamed a continent in breathtaking speed, and an inventiveness that was a blessing to all mankind. But, by the same token, each increase in the individual's capacity to thumb his nose at custom and restraint brought a corresponding decline of community and those bonds of respect and trust and shared value that bind atomistic souls into a cordial unity. As long as there was a certain balance between centrifugal individualism and centripetal community the world prospered and the two complimented each other—the individualists innovating, while the community stabilized and added value. The community still retained its healing power to care for the needy, share and enforce values, and repress dangerous or outlandish things. But this felicitious balance has been smashed and individualism now reigns so triumphant that community scarcely exists. There are few shared values. No shared religions, or experience. Nothing that is widely venerated. Patriotism, a key aspect of community value, is virtually dead, scorned if not hated by the atomistic individuals in the intelligentsia. There is some neocommunal life in the form of clubs to promote various entertainments such as dune buggying or chess or horse raising and showing. But these are no substitute for the deeper sense of belonging to a nation, or state, or town, or culture, that once imbued the thinking of most Americans. There is no pride in us. So rampant is today's individualism that it threatens to atomize even the smallest communities which we know as families. The divorced rate is an expression of an individualism that no longer accepts the restraints of the common good or venerates old values. The commandment, "love thy neighbor," is almost forgotten because we have no neighbors—only strangers in the apartment next door. A large segment of our population now functions as atoms, unattached to any deep value or place or nation or God. Their restlessness is a significant force in an America that has lost its organic center. The trade unions have supplied some sense of community to some workers; the trade associations and proliferating interest groups provide some adhesion for others. And, of course, the Christian community persists, even in the face of an atomized, scientized world.

During much of its early renaissance, American conservatism was seduced by the older liberal individualism and the proposition that dismantling the state and adding to personal liberty would cure much of what is wrong to America. There was even the name of the conservative theoretical and intellectual organization, the Intercollegiate Society of Individualists (renamed in 1966 the Intercollegiate Studies Institute), to ratify the liberal mystique of rampant individualism as the curative force in America. That conservatism—at least its traditionalist wing—has now escaped that trap is the result of one man's insight. Russell Kirk's rich portraits of an atomistic society governed by coercive state institutions had an enormous impact on the early right. It was Kirk who floodlighted the evanescent voluntary community and its voluntary authority as a fruitful force in life, and a social infrastructure that enables each of us to find a comfortable niche. It was Kirk who pointed to statist collectivism as the dark power that would flood into the vacuum left by disintegrating norms and communal feelings. It was Kirk who drew the first horrifying picture of atomistic individuals responsible to nothing, venerating nothing, governable only through stark coercion. It was Kirk who pointed to liberalism in both its current statist and older libertarian guises as the force that demolished the social cohesion of the Christian West in the name of liberty.

But now, Kirk's ideas are not popular within much of conservatism, and especially among the libertarian young. Businessmen and freedomists alike cling to the older liberal belief that any authority, even the most gentle and benevolent type, is bad authority and that the authority of government, especially, is eroding individuals into becoming mass men. Indeed one branch of conservatism sees not a rampant individuality as the threat, but a rampant state on the verge of snuffing out the last vestiges of individuality in anyone and turning the whole society into rubber-stamp personalities. This thesis is superficial, and lays all the blame on the state even though innumerable other social factors are involved.

One of the ironies of becoming an atomized individual without allegiances is that there is a simultaneous draining away of character, or true individuality. To the extent the authority of community is destroyed, so, too, is the individuality of the atoms freed from social norms. Community and individuality are, in the end, inseparable and indispensable to one another. Community—the voluntary association of people for common causes—is the great barrier to the coercive collectivist state, and with the destruction of community and its norms and morals there must follow inevitably the influx of coercion. Nowhere is this more manifest than in the youth cults that now grind away at the vestiges of norms while fostering collectivist and coercive social arrangements both as part of, and to follow, their revolution. The gentle strictures of community opinion were too much even for these raging individualists; they are obsessed with shredding even the churches because they preach moral and ethical restraints.

The earlier individualism had a positive impact: it liberated minds from stifling myths and ruts. It freed persons to overcome feudal passivity and make their lives fruitful. It established widespread private ownership and formed the basis of a free society with voluntary contractual arrangements to bind men together. But it also, in the end, was hurtful to those social ties that men need to live together, and finally it fostered more and more radical cults and movements: Greenwich Village nonconformists first, which were tolerated easily. Beatniks, hippies, drug cultists, and now Weathermen and Black Panthers, which are not assimilable at all, and must be resisted as a matter of preservation. All this evolution can and should be laid at the feet of liberal tradition: it is the fruit of an obsession with individuality and nonconformity.

Those liberals who concede the validity of a conservative tradition in the West sometimes use the analogy of the brake pedal on a speeding car to describe the proper social function of conservatism. They regard conservatism as the social force that impedes progress when change is too rapid. Another function ascribed to the right by its enemies is the consolidation and administration of liberal gains. In this viewpoint, progress is always leftward, but occasional periods of conservatism are needed to purify liberal experimentation and make it more efficient, and provide the footing for new liberal advances once the existing programs are soundly

153

embedded in the government structure. This was the mission the liberals of both the Republican and Democratic parties assigned to the Eisenhower administration. The theory is exquisitely self-serving and not a little arrogant. It assumes a linear historical progression leftward; the total rightness of progress in a single direction, and the bankruptcy of any non-leftist ideas. It assumes that conservatism is, at best, a method of purifying liberal schematics. It assumes conservatism accepts the basic tenets of liberalism, including the tenet of gradual accretion of power to the state, the increasing secularization of society, and the increasing size of the public sector and taxation.

But conservatism accepts none of these hypotheses; indeed, the conservative consensus is so radically at odds with liberal presumptions that liberals instinctively foster a phoney tame right (e.g., the late Clinton Rossiter) who are to be the "house niggers." The real conflict between liberals and conservatives centers on the ideology of progress. There is no certitude within the conservative tradition that history is evolving toward a worldly paradise. Although conservatives concede a quantum jump in the sum total of knowledge, the accretion of knowledge is not necessarily equatable with progress except in a limited fashion, such as in technological comforts. The history of the twentieth century confounds the whole idea of progress and suggests that man's nature contains a barbarism that is not excised by democracy, or science, or education, or cybernetics, or psychology, or, for that matter, any human discipline. The more sensitive liberals know it, and their writings no longer express the bustling optimism of two centuries of earlier liberalism. The question of progress hinges not so much on technological advance as it does on human nature, which is still capable of deploying the technology for good or evil; to build or destroy; to free or imprison. Any progressive vision must include as a central thesis the idea of man's ultimate goodness; his evolution toward sainthood, even if it were some sort of secular sainthood. The versions of progress cannot support the idea of an unchanging human nature, greedy and vicious. In the era of the John Dewey cult it was supposed that education was the key. Psychologists sought the key in behaviorism. And now cybernetics and science, and even mood-elevating drugs to dope the evil out of us. This long, dismal procession of shattered liberal hopes suggests human nature is much less tractable to worldly cures than the earlier liberals supposed, and now it appears liberals are prepared to drug us to create their earthly paradise. Peace will be the flowering of a stupefied, tranquilized humanity. "Have you had your pill today?" will no longer be an amusing college poster joke, but a state edict.

The liberals who are so fond of asserting the world is changing have sup-

154

posed that change is virtually always desirable, although the bulk of mankind has historically—and with some validity—thought change to be as frequently undesirable or ruinous. The constant reiteration that the world is changing is as much a liberal wish-ritual as it is an observation, and somehow always leans toward the concrete realities of scientific advances, and rarely toward the terrible intractability of the human spirit. Conservatives take a more sanguine approach to history as something epochal or cyclical, and devoid of transcendent terrestrial goals such as are embedded in the dream of a United Nations godhead. The conservative viewpoint is altogether shocking, if not unbearable, to the left. History must move upward, at least in the Hegelian dialectical sense of two steps forward for every one backward—or else life is without meaning! That's it exactly. For the liberal, whatever meaning appertains to his existence for three score years and ten, rests in the hope that he will leave the race better than he found it.

The conservative intuition suggests that life has another dimension located in religion and in the plan of a transcendent God. The alternative to the teleology of progressive history is not stasis, not a period of dark ages and total otherworldliness, but the expansion of the kingdom of the King of Kings in the hearts of men. Human nature has shown itself tractable to one reforming force: the Christ. It is this insight that must force the libertarian wing of the right ultimately to fall away and join the left. The libertarian thesis rests on a vision of society in which progress is produced by liberating man both economically and morally from the past. Its neo-laissez faire is one of the liberal visions of secular utopia. It rests on a linear vision of historical progress wrought through man's unaided intelligence and endeavor. And so, although there is a deep libertarian instinct in orthodox conservatism, at bottom the premises vary and there can be no more than an alliance of convenience for a space of time. Even now, in the defections of libertarian economist Murray Rothbard to the New Left, in the abandonment of Young Americans for Freedom by a sizable libertarian wing, in the deepening animosity of the Ayn Randian Objectivists toward conservatives, there is an unhealed schism that can no longer be bridged.

The conservative is the true skeptic about secular reforms, and his sense of history informs him of the futility of all those programs created by hopeful progressives, who pull illusion onto delusion in their struggles to tame mankind. Man is not tameable except through grace—that is, except through obedience to, and faith in, the Master. But even grace is a gift, bestowed by God. The spreading of grace is the enterprise of the orthodox church, and the success of the mission is evident in the publication of the

155

gospel in all lands. Grace is ameliorative; that is, the man who lives his Christianity is concerned about others—not in an abstract liberal way, such as sending food to abstract and unknowable Biafrans half a world away—a noble gesture, of course, but an odd one considering the sorrows so close at hand. Rather, grace is a force that turns the abstract welfarism of liberals into a fiery commitment and positive love toward those nearby. "Love thy neighbor" turns out to be exactly that, and is the main worldly obligation of Christians. Neighbors are concrete, knowable people with personalities and antagonisms and problems, rather than mere abstract recipients of abstract benevolence, however well-intentioned. The food, of course was not abstract, and it saved Biafran lives. But that is not the point. The scheme of liberal benevolence is the point; the scheme that dealt with human digits rather than people. Conservatism deals with a more tangible, palpable world, and with a more transcendent overview of man and his destiny, expressed in the love of God.

13. PURITANISM

THE history of the Congregational church has significant things to say about the decline of religion, and about Puritanism, which the secular kids hate above all else. It is the story of freedom, brilliance, theocracy, a bit of fanaticism, and ultimately the near apostasy of a large segment of the modern church. The early Separatists rebelled against the popishness of the Church of England, and believed that they could find a holier, simpler, less ritualistic Christianity based on Scripture. They fled to the New World to establish Massachusetts Colony, a New Zion, a bold experiment in which God Himself would be the guiding force. The Congregational church had no hierarchical structure, and congregations were autonomous. To this day they select their ministers and govern themselves through the equivalent of a town meeting. The Puritans established a theocracy in the New World in which religion was not only a moral and spiritual reality but also a social and governmental one, too. Religion pervaded the inner and outer lives of the Puritans. The church was liberal: that is, it was grounded in the brilliant insight that if the canons, rote and ritual of formal priestly religion were stripped away, so that man's conscience could be guided directly by God through scriptural authority, a community of saints would emerge; a New Zion, the City of God on earth. It was a magnificent idea. In an age when Christian religion scarcely percolated in any meaningful way to the mass of men, the early Congregational church lifted the barriers. If a man or a woman could read or hear, he or she could be instructed in the Word of God and live accordingly. Early in its history the church evolved a brilliant clergy which probed and explored every facet of man's relation with God and Jesus Christ. The liberalism of the church initially produced congregations closer to the Christian ideal than anything seen in Europe. To be sure, that liberalism also evoked a thread of fanaticism, but that fanaticism is overdrawn by modern secular historians. If the Puritans did hang some witches, it was less an instance of specifically Puritan intolerance than the stamp of an era of fierce religious conflict in which heretics and others were slaughtered by the legion. If anything, the liberalism of the New World Puritans mitigated the religious holocausts that were sweeping through the Old World. Nor was the Puritan life as grim as some historians wish to portray it. While church services were lengthy, often involving a sermon of several hours duration in an unheated building, they were often extremely interesting and richly illustrated, thanks to the brilliance of the ministry. If there were some hellfire and damnation, there was also a lilting melody of love and rejoicing. The Puritans were not an unhappy, dour people. There were love and community and a deep sense of participating in an emerging new order. Consciences were well developed; there was a moral structure, a framework snugly enclosing life, that minimized crime, theft, moral disorders, and madness. If anything, the liberal spirit of the church—the freedom to move ever closer to God, freely seeking and learning without the terrible impediments of hierarchy—produced one of the most genuinely Christian societies in the long procession of Christian experiment. The Congregational churches moved from glory to glory. The church founded Yale and Harvard and supplied its fertile ministry from the fine divinity schools it had established. The plain, white, Congregational churches, prim and lovely in their simplicity, began to dot the whole of New England even as the Episcopal church spread through Virginia and the South. The Puritan character grew, in time, less otherworldly and more hard-headed, and by the time of the revolution the Puritan church was the spiritual shepherd of a race of traders, intellectuals, and yeoman farmers.

But the theological liberalism that had originally blossomed into the most intense Christianity contained the seeds of trouble. Conscience is rubbery in a church without hierarchy or canon. By the time of the great Brahmins—Emerson, Thoreau, the Adams family, Oliver Wendell Holmes, and Longfellow (whose intellectual traditions were a heritage of the Congregational Church)—the brilliant ministry was experimenting with novel doctrine, the most significant being the Unitarian one, in which the divinity of Christ is essentially rejected, even though Jesus is seen as a man

158

infused with special goodness. A large segment of the Congregational church decamped to the Unitarians, and the Unitarians have retained their position of being the least orthodox of any of the faiths; indeed, have, in large measure, converted to an ethical humanism devoid of any belief in a divine being. But the same freedom, the same dependence exclusively on scripture and conscience that had earlier worked prodigies of faith in the Puritan churches, began increasingly to work in the opposite direction until today, except for a splinter group, most Congregational churches are at the vanguard of the secular left-liberal enterprise. Many of the churches, heeding the siren song of the social gospel and ecumenicism, decamped to the new United Church of Christ, although there remained a significant number of Congregational churches that continued in the old tradition. As usual, the congregations voted freely which direction they would go; and, as usual, there was dissension. The irony of ecumenicism-by-majority rule is that it broke the Congregational church in two, and even broke individual congregations into splinters.

While the Congregational churches still retain their brilliant ministry and the sermon is still the central—and most intellectual—part of the worship service, most Congregational churches reverberate to the catchwords of the Peace and Freedom movement; to pulpit harangues for welfarist measures; to an easing of moral and theological rigors; to a preoccupation not with struggling souls of communicants, but with social engineering of society. There has been a massive tinkering with the liturgy. The great hymnals are lying in disuetude and mod kids with guitars occupy pulpits. Laymen "participate" more frequently, and "relevance" is commonly stressed, even though relevance is often a mask for the abandonment of the teachings of Jesus. Parts of the Congregational Church are a theological shambles and are approaching a moral shambles as well. The congregations are, as with so many mainline Protestant congregations, increasingly grayhaired. In some Congregational churches the message is pure secular humanism clothed in the mantle of a distant, abstract, pantheistic God who is described as nothing more than reality. If there were apostasy in the Congregational churches, it has been led principally by the ministry rather than the more orthodox congregations. In a free church, the most novel interpretations of scripture find equal status with older, tested interpretations. A William Sloane Coffin can zoom off on his own tangent and there is no orthodoxy to stop him. There is no heresy in a free church. There is nothing more binding than a simple test of sincerity. Perhaps the true tragedy of Congregationalism is that its liberal ministers have ceased ministering. They are liberal polemicists, with the hubris of the intellectual and the self-righteousness of the revolutionary. The church's sermons have

159

been its glory; today, they are frequently its shame. The freedom and boldness with which the Congregational ministry developed its themes, based on scriptural texts, have always astonished both Catholics and fundamentalist Protestants who chanced to hear a Congregational sermon. But now the babble of ideology emerges from the pulpits.

However, there are several points about this freedom worth stressing. Within the church there are strong orthodox congregations and ministers who have abandoned nothing, and who continue steadfastly in the beliefs of traditional Christianity. The same freedom that has permitted so much experimentation also permits orthodoxy. Nor is the virtual apostasy of portions of the church ascribable only to the freedom and autonomy of the church. The structured churches are all experiencing the same turmoils: each has its Berrigan brothers, Father Groppi, Bishop Pike, or Harvey Cox. The presence or absence of structure and dogma seems to have little to do with the agonies afflicting modern churches. One can chance a few intuitive guesses about the causes. It is clear that something is eroding Christian tradition in both the free churches and the dogmatic ones, and it is clear that a hierarchy, dogma, and catechism are no proof at all against every conceivable theological novelty. One might well suppose that the churches are fighting those "powers and principalities" of evil that were remarked by St. Paul. Or one could suppose that we are witnessing the great falling away prophesied by Jesus in his description of the last days.

There is, within Congregationalism, an approach to religion that is most difficult to describe adequately to communicants of the highly structured churches. Among the most devout ministers there is a quest to reach closer to God, even if that means examining some of the old creeds and questioning the dogma of the early councils. There is suspicion among free church ministers that the rote formulas are sometimes inadequate, if not erroneous. The result is often sermons that enrich and enlarge the central Christian experience. That is, in a sense, theological liberalism, but it is using the freedom of conscience and intellect in the way the early Puritans did; to find new avenues and explanations; to find a richer faith, obedience, and joy in the Christian experience. For those who have experienced this theological liberty, the spiritual advancement is sometimes breathtaking, and Christian belief forms an ever-deepening meaning in the lives of the fortunate. Clergymen of the structured churches scarcely concede such a phenomenon is possible without plunging into dire heresies. For it has been commonly noted the Christian heresies usually spring from excessive zeal rather than from abandoning the faith. There is no formal heresy in the free church but there is always the chiding of God. There is

160

no human intermediary to say nay, but there is the pang of conscience and the authority of the Bible.

One of the great curiosities of our secular times is that today, three centuries after the heyday of Puritanism, those early Separatists and their ideals are the single most abused and despised group in the history of the United States. Nearly every one with some pretensions of intellect blames Puritanism for virtually every evil, disorder, and cruelty besetting the Republic. Puritanism is blamed for every private hang-up plaguing individuals. Puritanism is even blamed for much of what is wrong (or right) in the economy and business world. (Indeed, it was voguish in the early '60s to call federal budget-balancing economic Puritanism!) Puritans, moreover, are continually blamed for things not of their making, such as Victorian squeamishness about naming body functions, or Victorian ultramoralistic and hypocritical sex attitudes. Even within the Congregational churches, direct linear descendants of the whole Puritan culture, "Puritanism" is regularly denigrated by mod ministers seeking relevance with the kids. No matter where one moves through mod society—from *Playboy* to the *New York Review of Books*—that is, from the ridiculous to the sublime—Puritanism is a devil-word, a devil concept. Moreover, there is ascribed to Puritanism a catalogue of evils that are greatly exaggerated—fanaticism, for example. While there were periods of fanaticism within Puritanism, such as that which drove Roger Williams to Rhode Island, Puritanism was still a doctrine of love and mercy and salvation. Puritan virtues aren't honored, except sentimentally around Thanksgiving. But it is not recorded that the Puritans were unhappy, or mad, or vicious, or criminal, or uncharitable. On the contrary, it is clear that the Massachusetts Colony was noted for its stability, honesty, and industry, and the felicity of life extracted from a stony soil. The Puritan vision of a New Zion is scarcely remembered now, though the word *Puritan* is the hate-word of our times.

The Puritans were, above all, moralists, and perhaps that is why secular men revile them. Morals are the least tolerable medicine that secular men must swallow. Their tactic has been reductio ad absurdum—the moral rigors of Puritanism have been described with such harshness that no reasonable men could uphold them. It is natural for the secularists to pick the richest symbol of Christian morality and assail it, and so Puritanism lives today as the thing most hated by the run of men, even though there is scarcely an authentic Puritan alive. The Puritans were, in George Santayana's phrase, moral aristocrats, and this was not because of endless codes of conduct enforced with Pharisee vigor, but because the Puritans

161

were endlessly attempting to become spiritual man, and to discard the carnality of the natural man. The disciplining power in Puritanism was not negative but positive: the hunger through the whole community for union with God. It is plain that by the time of Nathaniel Hawthorne those hungers had been codified into powerful social mores that had intolerant aspects. (A lack of charity was one of the weaknesses of Puritanism.) But despite these troubles, the Puritans were a remarkably vigorous, moral, and happy people, and the viciousness of the current assault on these long-gone people suggests modern envy. Puritanism now seems to be nearly synonymous with the word, *principled,* and if that were the case, there are some on earth who should be wearing the pejorative word with pride and honor. Indeed, to be a Puritan today is to live in joy and holiness and love.

14. CAPITALISM / SOCIALISM

THE true revolutionary force loose in the world today is capitalism; and, in a sense, we are all reactionaries trying desperately to cope with the deluge of innovations and social changes that flood from the capitalist system. The hip kids, no less than the liberals and conservatives and non-political people, are forced continually to defend old values, old status quos, endangered by radical capitalism. Within a few decades the consciousness and mobility of man have leaped upward so radically that no one quite comprehends what is happening. It is ironic that business entrepreneurs who are labeled reactionaries by the left are, in fact, promulgating a revolution so drastic that the left is breathlessly trying to catch up with it. The kids in particular sense the revolutionary impact of capitalism and their folk songs express yearning for a more settled, pastoral society without exotic change.

Capitalism fosters and exploits science and has developed the golden technology to alter radically the earth and change human relationships. So rapid is the evolution that whole professions—such as flight engineers—blossom and die in decades. Radical capitalism builds mushrooming cities in one locale while it permits others to wither away. The market economy, for all the abundance and price competition, also can be brutal and baffling. It may cause a manufacturer to pull up stakes and move to a locale where there are better markets leaving behind a bewildered, dying community. Radical capitalism may even build whole new communities: a Levittown here, a Huntsville there. Radical capitalism put wheels under our populace, built numerous motels to house our gypsies. It built four-wheel drives to penetrate our remaining wilderness.

Radical capitalism gouges our mountains for minerals; builds giant harvesting machines that drive superfluous rural populations into cities. Radical capitalism develops seed strains infinitely more fruitful than earlier ones; it pushes huge roads through canyons and mountains. Suburbs mushroom while the city cores wither, thanks to the innovative power of free capitalism. Those who mastered a skill they supposed would last a lifetime must now relearn it and relearn it again.

Amidst this great roar of machines and economic expansion, individuals find themselves hungering for a simpler, unchanging existence. Rarely do they comprehend that capitalism, not communism, is what is disrupting and overturning their lives and forcing new values on society, and new social arrangements. Radical capitalism, for example, often moves executive families every few years all over the nation: the parents thus are stripped of the older comforts of lifelong friends, or life in a settled, comfortable, familiar neighborhood. The kids are ripped so often from their young companions that they learn not to have deep friends at all, but to stay armored, to stay cool. Radical capitalism has its own evil side effects: neon jungles, or highway strip cities garishly competing for the last dime. The older aesthetics have been demolished by dynamic capitalism along with the quietude and tranquility of earlier eras. To be sure, there has been a cornucopia of abundance spewing down even to the lower classes for the first time in history, and capitalist technology has been able to bring medicine and health within reach of most people. But all this has been at terrible cost: the old verities are demolished, the old neighborhoods bulldozed; the old religion lost; the old spatial sense expanded, the old poetry and art disintegrated, the old silence drowned out—and the older peace ruined. Radical capitalism acccounts for the desperate hunger to preserve some remaining slices of the silent wilderness to escape into. It underlies the ecological wars of our time. The dynamism of capitalism so outstrips the dynamism of any other social arrangement that liberals spend much of their energy trying to slow it down, to harness the unleashed monster that is hot-dogging and hog-rooting the world. Most of the liberal programs in Congress are actually reactionary—they are desperate reactions to the untamed machine of free enterprise capitalism. Those much-scorned businessmen are riding the horses of the apocalypse and the much-vaunted progressives are applying all the brakes they can muster. These slowing processes are innumerable and seek, at bottom, to ameliorate the psychic disruption, the spiritual shocks of the racing capitalist leviathan. Recently, to take one minute example, Congress gave tax breaks to those who move—a recognition that a man's career now careens around the Republic and that business benefits from a more fluid labor supply. Consciously or unconsciously, the legislators intend to slow the monster down. New pollution laws require proper controls over by-products. New real estate development laws in some states require innumerable tests of good faith and quality and proper planning. The legislatures of the several states, the whole bureaucracy, the federal government, Congress, and various pro bono groups, are all engaged in lassoing the mad bull of capitalism; in building roadblocks against entrepreneurs.

The kids see it all in simpler terms. Amidst the roar of capitalist machines they hunger for lullabies. They hear the Brahms lullaby, crystalline in its tranquility, on an old music box, juxtaposed against the roar of the freeways and snarling trucks. The kids remember the quiet flap of a sail out on a quiet lake; the peace of the deep woods. They gather in the New Mexico communes for the silence and to revive a way of virginal life almost untouched by capitalist revolution. The kids feel that Marxist and collectivist economics are less fruitful, but they intuitively prefer the stolid evolution and straitjacket of a collectivist state to the quicksilver disruptions of capitalism. They have not forgotten the lullabies; and they know a neighborhood ought to be a place where their parents can sink roots and live stable, established lives, secure in their own nests, with decades-old friends at every hand. To the pure economist who sees, for example, food costs as a declining part of personal income, and who sees supermarkets providing an unheard-of array of good and exotic taste treats from all over the globe, all fresh and unspoiled, the ingratitude of the kids is baffling. To him, enterprise capitalism is a magic carpet of abundance and universal comfort and blessing. But the pure economist rarely comprehends the aesthetic or social price; especially the price of impersonal living and the rupture of old neighborhoods. He thinks the kids' hatred of capitalism is some wild perversity.

The liberal progressives are less honest. They conceive of themselves as the progressive force; capitalism and businessmen as the reactionary force, even while the bulk of liberal reforms are reactions to capitalist innovations. It was not progressives who provided rising living standards or broader distribution of wealth; capitalism did it in one brilliant thrust since World War II, despite heavy bleeding by the state to provision wars and welfare. In the breathtakingly short span of a quarter of a century capitalism literally lifted the Republic to double and triple its previous in-

165

come levels and ushered in undreamed of miracles such as symphonies for anyone on LPs at home, or TV, or reliable cars cheap enough so that many families have two or three. To suggest that this was the work of the state, or the fruit of progressive-socialist ideology, is grotesque. The organizing genius of this upthrust was vested in men who loathed state power and regulation; who feared the redistribution of income by the state would deprive them of the capital necessary for new enterprises. To be sure, at some levels businessmen have sought state aid: that is, have tried to skewer the free market system that permitted the entrepreneurial mind to triumph in what is a modern demonstration of Adam Smith's invisible hand (Smith argued that the entrepreneur pursuing his private advantage for profit benefits the public weal with an invisible hand, creating jobs, cheaper and better products, national wealth, etc.). Business has sought protective tariffs, state-guaranteed monopolies, cartels, public loans and guarantees, and a myriad other interventions that inhibit the play of market forces. In most instances, liberals have acquiesced, with dubious results.

The shock of change proves to be too much for the alienated kids and they hate capitalism precisely because it is so dynamic. The stodgy certitudes of collectivist systems are somehow more comforting. But the kids have their labels wrong. Capitalists, not Weathermen, are the radical ones. Capitalism is uprooting older, settled traditions; not Weathermen. If the Weathermen bomb, it is to stop the machine—scarcely a revolutionary approach. But capitalism isn't stopping; it is chafing at the reins, wanting to move still faster, topple old ways even quicker. It wants to subdivide the West, put two cars in every garage; supply better, cheaper foods; jet myriads of people to romantic islands.

The true radicals in American society—indeed, the only authentic radicals—are the libertarian conservatives, the proponents of laissez faire. A truly free economy is the one unthinkable doctrine opposed alike by every branch of the left and center and some of the right. The libertarians are the ones who want to ride the capitalist tiger, who sense the impact for good in the capitalist revolution and in free entrepreneurs operating without restraint, revving up the business cycle. These are the ones who view Japanese capitalism, the runaway economic power on the globe, with a sense of benign satisfaction. Capitalist Japan, starting from the ruins of World War II, now outstrips socialist England and welfarist West Germany and has the entrepreneurial brilliance to overhaul the supereconomies, including that of the United States, with new affluence cascading upon the Japanese people.

Every other political group—socialists, Fabian progressives, liberals, old and new leftists, moderates, and, to some extent, traditional con-

166

servatives—seek, or acquiesce in, new ways to rein down radical capitalism. That is not what their rhetoric says, of course. They couch their manifestoes in different terms, filled with the promise of growth and spreading of income. They assail slow growth rates and the deep margins between rich and poor. But the effect of all their public policy is undeniably to slow things down. Pollution controls, consumer legislation, excess profits taxes, corporate income taxes, antitrust legislation, regulation of fuels, transport, and utilities, all impose a heavy and exacting burden on industries and products, and raise prices. Safety standards, work standards, NLRB protection of unions, minimum wages, and a host of other factors, each, in the end, clip the wings of soaring capitalism, for good or ill. The point here is not whether these reforms are valid, but rather that their true impact is to harness dynamic capitalism. It is, plainly, increasingly difficult to start a new business because of the rat's nest of red tape and licenses and trouble the government creates. Not even the government's subsidizing tactics—deferred taxes, loans, city industrial parks, etc., compensate for the growing maze of difficulties a new entrepreneur must negotiate.

One could, perhaps, argue that technology and science are the revolutionary forces in the world, rather than capitalism. But the socialist economies have been unable to translate science into products that reach and benefit the mass of men. Capitalism alone has the dynamism to grasp each scientific and technical advance and apply it in ways that have an immediate impact on consumers. Much of the progress, say, in photography has been the work of capitalists who finance the research that produced fast films, Polaroid, good color processes, reliable processing, microfilm storage, etc. These have scientific roots but the science was spurred by the quest for profit.

The old liberal and socialist argument that collectivist enterprise would be more efficient and would avoid wasteful competition is muted now, rather an embarrassing relic of the prewar years. The postwar demonstration of capitalism, especially in Japan, the United States, and West Germany, as compared to the lethargic behavior of socialist economies, simply laid the earlier hopes for socialism to rest, and progressives now view a mixed economy or a fascist-type economy (heavy state regulation of nominally private business) as the ultimate solution. A number of economic programs now advanced by liberals such as John Kenneth Galbraith were pioneered by Mussolini fascism and Hitler national socialism. In fascist Italy free competition was abandoned and the nation's industry and commerce were organized into a score or so of giant cartels. Each government corporation in Mussolini's corporative state had a political

167

overseer at the apex, empowered to control wages and prices within the monolithic structure, rather as President Nixon's Phase II Boards. It was de facto socialism even though titles remained vested in private entrepreneurs. In effect the state—or Fascist party—simply ran business and, by establishing price and wage policy, guaranteed that the cartels would neither succumb to competition nor gouge consumers. Nazi Germany—under the National Socialists—went farther leftward and did seek to socialize such businesses as banks and some retail stores. It, too, established rigid control over ostensibly private enterprise and established a massive welfare state. Nazi welfarism was once the envy of a horde of New Dealers until it became evident that it was an integral part of a totalist structure aimed at subjugating every facet of private life. This Nazi-type economy now is being promoted in the United States by a cynical combine of businessmen who fear competition and statist liberals who welcome any advance in public power.

Both systems gave the state extraordinary power over the economic well-being of private citizens, including the power to create or revoke jobs. It is axiomatic that a man's economic independence is his last refuge from an arbitrary and coercive state. Destroy his economic freedom, his right to win a raise, to save, buy, invest—destroy these and the victims are totally at the mercy of the political authorities. Economic freedom is one of the essentials of civil liberty: the two cannot be separated, not even by docile democratic socialism in which the individual supposedly has the political power to alter his state-decreed economic status. In this respect, free capitalism is the only system that guarantees the full liberty and opportunity of private citizens and permits them to evolve their lives according to their skills and determination. Socialism is inherently egalitarian and its politics dampen the enterprise of the most skillful and fruitful citizens except for the handful that achieves success within the ruling elite.

Socialism offers the kids some comforts that are stripped away by capitalism. If offers freedom from competition. At some level, the young people comprehend how horribly weak they are, seduced by their lusts, undisciplined, rarely able to apply themselves to any enterprise for any significant period. The career-oriented young people, conversely, still retain the old values that begin with self-mastery, and they know they can progress within the system. But the alienated youths know full well they are economic parasites, incapable of supporting themselves even if they didn't alienate their employers. To the extent they can work at all, it is usually in the public service sector utilizing tax monies or philanthropic revenue. The young radicals find slots in the academy, or in such agencies as VISTA or the poverty bureau, or in some schools (especially in slum

168

areas which other teachers shun), and in low clerical work. The economic future of the hip kids is perilous and deeply frightening to many of them. They hate the capitalists who could feed them. Subsidizing parents don't live forever, nor does their patience last forever.

The rage of the young against the "system" is, in some measure, the result of slamming doors. Few businesses willingly hire those who hate business, who even hate the necessity of earning their daily bread. Few alienated youths even wish to work; to do so is to surrender to corruption. They prefer, if necessary, to "rip off" what they need, which is a way of taxing the rest of us, through higher prices to cover losses. The collectivist economies thus become the focus of hope for the helpless hothouse flowers of the kid cults. Socialism becomes the salvation of their worthlessness, though very few of them have ever been honest enough to reduce their ideology to such personal terms.

In between the alien kids and the fruitful people who accept capitalism, there is a large body of others who do manage to work and survive within the system, even while resenting it and agitating for socialist reform. A great many liberals and New Leftists fall into this category. These are the ones particularly motivated by envy: because they resent the work they do, they do it less well than competitive career people, and thus fall behind financially. And then their envy festers into a political force toward their goals. They become militant unionists; foment managerial rebellions, push for more holidays, more overtime, etc. The politics of "screw the corporation" is the politics of the deeply envious. Career people, in contrast, tend to believe the operation of any enterprise in a free capitalist society is perilous and that the enterprise must be guarded tenderly and diligently lest it fail. And if this requires longer hours than the employer asks, the career man gives them gladly. His attitude is essentially giving; his goal is to be an asset. It is ironic that such people, often brilliantly educated and honest entrepreneurs, are labeled corrupt and greedy by the alienated kids whose only object is to take. There is a rampant myth among the alienated that only vicious, corrupt, grasping, and tricky persons reach the top. But the reality is that most of those in higher management and higher government have given of their skills and talents with a dedication surpassing the financial rewards tendered by the organizations for whom they work. Capitalism is comfortless for the many who have failed, including the alienated ones. Capitalism tests, weeds, purifies; it separates the dross. It wounds vain, lazy creatures.

But all this is not to suggest that only the weak are at the bottom. Men of great courage and honor exist there too, victims of injustice, prejudice, racial victimization, injury, calamity, collapsed health; loss of loved ones.

But these are rarely the alienated. A good man can weather infinite catastrophe without petulantly blaming the system or supposing that he was bludgeoned down by universally corrupt managerial classes. The sophomoric accusations are no temptation at all to one who has character and ability to recognize calamity as the lot of most men at one time or another, and in one system or another. The very fruitfulness and opportunity of capitalism mocks the alienated, but for the worthy man, these supply hope and courage to try to restore life again or to build upward, however painfully and tediously. It is the foolish and corrupt who turn most readily to economic collectivism that will set safe boundaries around their lives, succor them no matter what their depravity, and remove the haunting, soul-gripping feeling of being inadequate to compete.

There is, of course, some validity in many of the criticisms of capitalism. There are deep corruption, kickbacks, theft, cheating, stock manipulation, milking of union funds, politicking for economic advantage. The corruptions of capitalism are especially apparent in secular business men, who now perhaps are in a majority, and in secular management, whose personal greed and ambition has burst out of the weakening boundaries of waning Christianity. Through the period of early capitalism, the church was a natural checkrein to keep entrepreneurs honest. In retrospect we look at early capitalists as exploitative, especially of labor, with ten- and twelve-hour days, children and women included, and pitiful pay. But these conditions were usually superior to the life on the farms of the era, where work never ceased and poverty was grinding. The flood of rustics to the factories was induced by superior, rather than inferior, opportunities and conditions. So profoundly Christian were many of the early entrepreneurs that they regulated employee conduct—and their own conduct—even to requiring prayers and guaranteeing the proper moral environment for lodging. The early capitalists may have imposed strenuous conditions, but they were often informed by Christian ethics and belief. The system was not corrupt, nor in general was it driven as much by greed as it is now. The alienated kids see the publicized greed in our modern system but they don't see the unpublicized generosity and dedication and public service of some businessmen and managers. Some kids suppose capitalism was always innately corrupt, but this supposition is based upon a serious misreading of history, and a liberal mythology about early capitalism that has been discredited thoroughly by economic historians. But the myth persists and forms one of the grounds for radical overthrow of the whole system. The kids are primarily informed by liberals who basically loathe capitalism, feel it is a necessary evil, and consider themselves whores of the establishment for accepting it. The young people sense the liberal embarrassment over capitalism and take the fateful step of rejecting it altogether rather than adopting the alleged prostitution of the liberals.

It would be difficult to argue any close correlation between Christianity and capitalism—at least not as long as Japan continues to blossom as the capitalist Cinderella. Nor would it be easy to maintain that secular men necessarily evolve toward collectivist approaches to economic organization. Karl Marx was a creature of the Christian West just as much as Adam Smith. There is much of the Christian attitude embedded in capitalism, but collectivism may be a special Christian heresy, evolving not so much from secular attitudes per se, but from disintegrated Christianity; disillusionment with Christian solutions; disappointment in the Christian vision of utopia.

Socialism has the quality of trying to grasp Christian virtues and institutionalizing them by brute force, or state coercion. Socialism also uses the state to attempt to evade Christian vices, such as greed, through the mechanism of the state. Those most attracted to socialism are the sensitive, disappointed ones who find nothing of consequence remaining in Christian mythology, but still live on the penumbra of Christian virtue; who believe, that is, that man ought not to be greedy and exploitative, and that the needy should be cared for, and that the rich should surrender their riches. Under a Christian régime these things are personal dicta and are voluntary. If it were morally right for the rich man to be generous with his abundance, at least there is nothing in Christianity compelling him to surrender his wealth. But socialism of all descriptions seeks to accomplish virtue by main force. It uses the state to mount a frontal assault on wealth, to confiscate it and put it to the beneficial use of the poor. In this sense, collectivist economics are a species of Christian heresy since they substitute state violence for the personal will.

But the vision of the state as the moral repository is very attractive to some people, especially the sensitive young who are acutely aware of the world's injustices. Socialism holds great promise for them: it will foil the crafty rich and bring their exploitations to naught: as with Christianity, it promises the last shall be first and the first shall be last. It offers not charity, but state-run welfare that shall secure the bodies and bellies and comforts of every citizen. And, of course, with the sovietization of industry the productive enterprises shall be run for the sole benefit of the workers rather than for the profit of the exploiters.

The collectivist view is shot through with a warped vision of Christian ideals and Jewish virtues. Christianity makes the poor and needy a personal responsibility; charity, indeed, is considered along with faith to be one of the essentials of Christian life. Socialism, erected in despair on the

171

apparent failure of the church, assumes the same responsibility for the poor but uses the state to rip off the necessary succor. Charity thus is transmuted into welfare and the poor receive their bread not as a matter of benevolence but as a matter of right. There are socialists who argue, indeed, that the living do have a right to succor, and that it is a moral lacuna in Christianity that it advocates no state-run system to keep people from starving.

When each of the old Christian virtues becomes vested in the collectivist state, it is no longer a virtue. Distribution of alms becomes a matter of collectivist technical skill rather than mercy. The state thus becomes the secular man's comfort; the relief of his conscience. The problem of starvation and misery around him is no longer his personal cross, but belongs to the omnicompetent state, and if he feels the state's dole is inadequate, he need not supplement from his own purse, but rather agitate for still more state redistribution. This is as true of our quasi-socialist programs, such as the poverty war, as it is of total communism. The managers of these state programs, of course, assume enormous power—indeed, the power to starve the unwanted or rebellious into submission. But socialists prefer that possibility over the alternatives of entrusting the poor to the mercy of God, or of Christians informed by God, or to sensitive businessmen.

There are, of course, many types of secular men, ranging from those who love Christianity and despair because they think it is a myth, to those who cynically reject every "repressive" moral and ethical tenet of the church and consider the sacred beliefs to be so much rubbish and hogwash. There are the ethical humanists who derive a moral code from portions of Christianity, and there is an expanding body of people purely secular, i.e., without any contact or consideration of spiritual belief; simple pagans. But the ones who are most deeply disappointed in the Christianity or Judaism of their fathers and who find the heavens empty and silent at a time of great tribulation, are those who are near the faith, but not quite in it. Some of the radicalized kids are of this sensitive, hurt, disappointed type, and they turn to socialism as a desperate substitute, well aware of its history of tyranny, but accepting that to the alternative of a world of moral laissez faire in which God no longer seems to intervene blessedly. Socialism is very close to being a religion in its own right. There is a clear reason why the communist state can't abide religion and considers it an archenemy.

There is described in Acts a brief experiment of early Christians in communal living and the sharing of "all things in common." It formed the basis of that hybrid flower called Christian Socialism. But what the modern exponents of socialism ignore is that this early sharing was not collectivist, but communal. It was voluntary. Those who wanted to withdraw could

172

and did. The giving into the central pool was not coerced by government and was, therefore, an act of private generosity, a surrendering of personal riches to Christ with all the spiritual advancement that implies. But modern socialist systems are not voluntary and involve no act of mercy or charity for the good of the soul. They function by exacting steep taxes or expropriating profits and thus, if anything, negate the unselfishness that the early Christians hoped and failed to achieve.

Capitalism, at least as it evolved in the West, has innumerable Christian attitudes embedded in it. There is nothing explicitly Christian about it, however; and it would be imprudent to argue that the capitalist system is divinely ordained. Indeed, for perhaps 1700 years Christianity prospered among a people whose economics were not capitalist at all, nor individualist either. But there are certain western economic traditions that are rooted in the faith. Basic personal honesty, free contract between individuals, the control of greed and envy, the doctrine of fairness and justice, are all essential to a proper capitalism. The Christian freedom to sin has implications that carry into a free market economy. Christianity creates and projects the autonomous individual free to accept or reject the church's moral teaching. There is no coercive effort to make the individual conform to high standards; at most, there is the warning of perdition. In the end it is up to the individual to make his own choices. This autonomy and free competence of individuals are also the cornerstone of capitalism and a free market. It forms the basis of the contractual relationship in which individuals voluntarily contract with each other to sell or buy, or pursue a common enterprise. In authoritarian and collectivist economies contracts play a surprisingly limited or nonexistent role. Stalin's daughter, Svetlana Alleluvia, who escaped to the United States, described her bewilderment in the face of a simple American publisher's contract, and her need to have the nature of contracts explained to her, along with the terms of enforcement. In one stunning and revealing sentence she revealed that in her entire life in the Soviet Union she hadn't signed a contract, and didn't know what one was.

The implications are profound. Rarely, if ever, does the Soviet citizen have so much as an opportunity either to bargain or to contract for any economic purpose. Obviously he buys, and purchasing is a simple contract. But the Soviet citizen has little contact with any entrepreneurial contract; he has lost his liberty to negotiate anything to his advantage; to covenant with any others than the state. The implication is that he has also lost his personal autonomy. The benevolent communist bureaus make his economic decisions for him, deciding even his options in the employment marketplace. While it is, no doubt, comforting to some to be freed of con-

173

tractual autonomy, it must chafe upon others to be so diminished and distrusted by the omnipotent Soviet state. The substitute mechanism for contract is bureaucracy. Soviet bureaus hold all the decision-making power and the Soviet citizen who seeks to change his status in any fashion does so by consulting with, and cajoling, the Deciders, rather than contracting with others freely to alter his life. Some of the most pointedly poignant of Miss Alleluvia's paragraphs deal with her heady, springtime discovery of our most humble liberties, such as those involving the free market and the concommitant discovery that the American state assumes she is competent to manage her existence.

It is difficult to say whether this heady freedom to manage one's life has Judeo-Christian roots. Probably it does. It is also probable that there is some correlation between secularism and the collectivist domination of the economic life of each person. There may be some loose empirical evidence that the more religious or Christian nations tend toward free-market and capitalist economies and the more secular ones tend toward collectivist economies. But there are innumerable difficulties, exceptions, and complications in that theory, including the different approaches to political economy fostered by Protestant, Catholic, and Orthodox Christianity. Certainly, in the United States, however, the secular citizens—with some exceptions such as Ayn Rand and her cult—lean toward collectivist economic programs while Christians—except the liberal variety—tend to group around a free market, private enterprise economy. But it would be perilous to extend the argument to Europe where there are such hybrids as Christian socialism and where national histories play a major role. In religious Poland communists rule. In secular England there is a mix, perhaps reflecting the conflict of older English values with the newer Fabian ones. Secular Sweden is still predominantly capitalist despite an enormous welfare state hooked to the capitalist dynamo, and secular West Germany entertains the same capitalist-welfare state mix.

A free market is grounded in trust. Contracting parties trust each other and believe thay can work for mutual advantage. Buyers trust the reputation of the seller. Buyers trust the quality controls and guarantees of the manufacturer. Sellers trust the financial viability of the buyers. Our entire credit system is a monument to the integrity of the vast majority of Americans, and could not function in a den of thieves. The trust is rooted, at bottom, in Christian training received by a majority of Americans; the evolution of a self-governing capacity in our citizens based on conscience and courage. The perfected Christian is a self-governing man, morally responsible and charitable; able to recognize his responsibility to others and be concerned over the well-being of those around him; able to care

174

about whether transactions are mutually beneficial rather than just beneficial to himself. All of his moral underpinnings that build a basic integrity into him—a middle-class morality, if you will—equip him to enter the free market and profit in it without hurting others; indeed, by helping others. This is Christianity's contribution to liberty and a market economy. Even now, after secularism has made deep inroads into religious conviction there remains the moral capital of Christianity vested in the mass of men, who still regard theft, deceit, greed, and envy as inherently evil. Our free market economy rests now on this dwindling moral heritage. But it is coming to rest more on social conformity which enforces right conduct, and on common law which also enforces right conduct, than on the older Christian power to send into the world a majority of citizens equipped inwardly to resist their own predatory instincts. As this Christian moral capital dwindles, so will the viability of free capitalism. As the middle-class morality dies, so, too, will our free market, because the predators will overcome the morally contained majority, and the plans for reform will center more and more on state regulation. The equation is simple: the less able the businessmen and consumers are to govern their appetites, the more the state must do it. As Christianity's authority dwindles, the state's waxes. A thoroughgoing collectivism is simply an expression of total distrust: consumers are not trusted to make the right decisions; producers and sellers are not trusted to function in the right way. The collectivist economics simply engulf and submerge the individual until he has no discretionary power over his very existence. And even if the collectivism were benevolent, as in the western democracies, it still operates to weaken and demoralize its subjects.

The kids recognize today's enterprise capitalism as a jungle, which it frequently is, even though the bulk of managers and capitalists remain among the most honorable of men. It takes only a minority of predators to blacken the whole system. The tragedy is that the alienated kids are turning toward Marxist-collectivist solutions which, in the end, demolish their own freedom and opportunity. Increasingly, they demand that corporations engage in various social and charitable activities, and produce higher quality goods. But business responsibility is not social awareness or any of the claptrap programs to turn profitable enterprise toward various species of community service. It is not the business of business to engage in community service but to make a profit and, thereby, guarantee jobs and good products in the marketplace. It is true that maximizing profits sometimes means lowering quality; but it is also true that maximizing profits sometimes means raising quality to a level of buyer acceptance. Quality, after all, is a factor that consumers are willing to compromise if it means cheaper prices. Not every consumer wishes to purchase a Rolls Royce; a serviceable car of medium quality is all he asks from the marketplace. To excoriate the free market for producing shoddy goods is to ignore the needs and the economic capacities of consumers. Competition raises product quality to a level of public acceptance and lowers product quality to a level of public acceptance.

In the main, the viability of free market capitalism rests on the morality of the entrepreneurs and consumers. The free market is an enormous policing force in its own right, but the free market cannot, in the end, substitute for the teaching, the power, and moral vision of Jesus Christ.

15. THE CHURCH GARRISONED

ON a tour of the San Francisco hippie districts a few years ago, Billy Graham discovered that, in some respects, the youngsters were spiritual pilgrims furiously at war with all that is corrupt in the square world. They lacked only God in their search for what is right and good. If they began with the sense that the world is unspeakably degenerate, that is not far from the Christian's own conviction that he must shun the world and serve God first. However, the kids not only lacked any communion with God, but also they were immersed in the same corruptions of body and spirit they hated so much in the square world. That is why a certain despair pervades the hippie districts: they could not even imagine a Christ who is their friend or who could help them out of their sorrows.

There exists in the hip kids the basis for a renewed Christian belief. They are not proud. They are not status-seekers as with so many American pharisees. They are not exclusive. Indeed, there is no other cohesive group in America that has so openly and kindly welcomed the freaks and weirdos who are usually outcasts buried alive in the hearts of the big cities. In the midst of the hip kids' consuming lusts and greed, in the midst of orgies and mysticism and downhill trips, there are acts of such incredible tenderness that they shame every square parent who believes the hip children represent the death of civilization. The freaks are not recorders or chroniclers, and so the world will have no record of the times when some wretched, stoned nymphet was taken to a crash pad, washed, fed, sheltered—and then urged to go back to the square world where hope still was alive. True, there are vicious hip types who recruit for the armies of lust and diabolism, but deep in the hip towns are strange angels who rearm the wretched to march out of hell and back to life. The angels are quietly at work among the lost and damned. Perhaps because God is fascinated by the lost, He is present more in Haight-Asbury than in the suburbs. One senses, somehow, that those who are labeled degenerate by the squares will march into the Kingdom of Heaven ahead of many of their accusers, who never wiped vomit off a lost child, or held hands with a freak, or sheltered the desperate and lonely.

Amidst the stinking decay of spirit and body in the rotting nests of the flower children and Radical Left, God is throwing his arms around all who cry to Him for help. Now and then a man or woman emerges from the subculture, a scared, humble, and altogether beautiful person who has seen and rejected hell and has something urgent to say about it. Some of them are the Jesus freaks, still enamoured of the acid-rock life but somehow changed and infused with a grace that permits them to resist their pot and porn, and discover within themselves a Spirit that keeps them from stumbling. They have an incredible courage: they speak boldly about their redemption to the mocking multitudes of hopheads, junkies, radicals, and crazies. Who among the straights has the courage to glory in God, and proselytize Christian belief even in the midst of diabolists? They are weak and wobbly, often with one foot out and one foot in their new life, but they find divine strength to totter into the pads of the lost and pray. The Jesus freaks are a great mystery. Some are lost and will drift away, but most will stumble out of perdition and begin their missions not only to the damned but also to all those virtuous ones whose hearts were never broken by temptation.

One of the reasons why the church will not die is that it remains a refuge for the troubled. It offers green pastures and still waters for those who were burned in the cauldrons of Babylon. There is not a miserable junkie in all of New York City, for example, who is not welcome to feast at the table of joy. Christian faith demands much—but offers still more. The evolution of a Christian character, as necessary and important as that may be, is in the end overshadowed by God's love and mercy for all the errant hearts that come to Him. No man who has experienced the divine love can forget it. The love is not based upon a bargain: "I'll be good so that you will love me." It is there, regardless of what one does or fails to do. It is there before birth and after death, a haven for the weary heart and broken spirit. That is what makes it a haven. If it were available only to those who

178

are clean and virtuous, it wouldn't be a refuge at all but a door slammed in the faces of the desperate, who cannot help what they are. Nor is the refuge just a place to lie wearily, relieved for the moment of the hot vices of the time. Rather, it is an outfitter of spiritual armor. A man finds not only refuge in divine love but also new strength, a new compass and map, and hope that extends beyond the wretched present to a beautiful future. It is the one retreat that leads to victory. Those are things that even devout Christians tend to forget. Our strivings to be better men are welcome; our faith in God's bottomless love is the key.

Even while the affluent squares drift from the cathedrals, content with their abundance and only mildly alarmed by the twilight civilization enshrouding them, the church well may be home to legions of hip kids who are struggling upward from hell on earth. Those scarred pilgrims, searching for some meaning to their drug and sex-sodden lives, will be more receptive to the welcoming hand of God than are the smug armies from the suburbs. That is the nature of the church: to welcome stray lambs while the others are not ignored but accepted as a matter of fact. The children of darkness will come, by ones and twos, down the long road to light, learning to forgive us at each way station. That is their task: to forgive all of us in the secure, square world who let them slip into oblivion. Their minds are veritable museums of unforgiven hurts; many of the prize exhibits are taken daily from glass cases and polished and dusted to remind them of the evils that drove them into a living death. The children will forgive, and in forgiving discover forgiveness; discover that they no longer hate themselves or the society that nurtured them, or their parents, or the United States, or whatever else the children of darkness hated in the days when they were old men in children's bodies.

Even as the kids drift home, there is a move among faithless fat clergymen to make the church more relevant to the carnal world. They hope to fill the pews by weeding out of Christianity that which does not seem important now, nearly two thousand years after the Christ. Just what is relevant is hard to pinpoint; but, by and large, relevance is a code-word for liberal social attitudes. It is relevant to talk in church about the evils of Vietnam, racism, and poverty. It is not relevant to sermonize about chastity, morals, the divinity of Christ, or the struggle to achieve good character. It is relevant to urge brotherhood as a high, abstract ideal; to introduce mod music into liturgy, to invite laymen to the pulpit, to ponder issues such as abortion, divorce, family life, or the unresponsiveness of American institutions. It is relevant to have rock concerts in church basements and hold jazz masses, or march to and fro between the denominations in a display of ecumenicism. But it is not relevant to discuss the Resurrection, or heaven, or hell. If possible, even the Easter message is to be toned down and made more palatable to skeptical parishioners.

Relevance is a mystery that seems to reside more in ideology than in faith. One thing is clear: the individuals who come hopefully, desperately, joyously, and dutifully to the pews to worship God aren't particularly relevant. So intent are the "relevant" ministers and priests upon renovating society that they scarcely minister to their own lonely, hungry flocks. Those people who find their way into the churches of the twentieth century are filled with hungers, lusts, hang-ups, joys, virtues, desperate needs, and disease—but how many relevant ministers have reached out to help them? So many ministers never even meet the persons they preach to—except when they die. It is their special damnation to say hopeful words over the coffins of men and women and children whom they never knew and about whom they never cared.

Implicit in relevance is the notion that some Christian belief is outmoded, for example, chastity. Mod kids don't want to be lectured about sex. They will not come to church to be warned against something they want desperately to try. So the clergy quietly puts aside that issue, and countless other issues and adopts a selective Christianity or even introduces concepts that are plainly non-Christian. To be sure, there are always social problems. But whether these yield to political solutions backed by the mod church, or yield only to the renewed spirit in individuals who are learning how to love, is the question. Implicit in mod religion is despair: the feeling that the traditional church has failed; that God failed; that orthodox religion has permitted evil to flourish. Implicit in some of the mod church is even a disbelief in God. The doctrine of relevance scarcely conceals the feeling that man is utterly alone, and must progress upward through his social arrangements and politics rather than through grace. Implicit in mod religion is the feeling that there is only one, brief, earthly existence and nothing beyond. Love, then, becomes a search for sensations. The church toys with sensitivity training, in fostering mutual emotional and physical gratification—but not in fostering joy.

With a few exceptions, the mod church does not seem to be gaining adherents. The pews are about as empty as they have been for years. The mod ministers can fill their plants with forums, rockfests, debates, and dialogues only to have the whole audience vanish into the night outside, untouched by God, his church, or the Holy Ghost. The relevant church is a whore.

It is true that expanding congregations do not necessarily indicate a church living in truth. Nor does the popularity of any church demonstrate that it is essentially Christian. The tenets of the faith are clear: those values cannot be used selectively. We have been promised that the church won't die. It may change drastically. There may be a great falling away; the hierarchies may collapse; the formal structure may crumble; the ecclesiastics may defect; but the church, defined simply as the body of believers, shall live, shall survive the rise and the fall of nations, empires, kings, presidents, and dictators. The church lives irrepressibly in the Soviet Union. The church survives in Eastern Europe and in Communist China, amid unspeakable persecutions. The church may survive even in America, amid luxury, unbelief, perversity, and worldliness.

Much has been said about the alleged burden the church imposes on secular men. But the question the church faces in the immediate future is the reverse: to what extent will the new secularism invade the ancient prerogatives of the church and hinder Christians and Jews from practicing their faith? There is no question but that the church will be harried by secular men, even as it is in that bastion of secularism, the Soviet Union. If there were no God, then the Houses of the Lord ought not to stand above the reach of the state: they ought to be taxed; indeed, taxed punitively to discourage people from fiddling with mythology and chicanery. If there were no God, then the charities run by the church ought to be taxed or commandeered so that they can form a part of the welfare state. Taxation is merely the obvious secular intrusion upon religion. In a collectivist society, the Gospel is treason. It is explicitly antisocial and dangerous to the stability of the state, and, therefore, worthy of eradication.

But long before such drastic measures become a reality in secular society, the religious family would feel intrusions in lesser ways. The school systems would stuff children with antireligious doctrine; parochial schools would cease to exist. Social conformity would function against Christian morals; against marital fidelity, against chastity; against Sabbath days. Far from imposing their will on others, devout men everywhere are sorely beseiged by the tidal wave of disbelief. Even now, no Christian is immune from the flood of secularism that is washing away the nation's spiritual life.

The more that the church falters as an institution, the more its failures will send shock waves into the hearts of its communicants. For those who have been taught that the church is almost synonymous with God, the collapse of hierarchical order will be traumatic. But to those who have grasped that the church is simply the body of believers, and not a hierarchy, the collapse of formal religion will not be a cause for despair, even if the organized church should vanish utterly. The true church would live still, all the purer for having been purged of its errors.

Increasingly, as secularism engulfs one bastion after another of the established faith, Christians will be tempted to break and run, or forget God, or abandon missionary endeavor. The church will garrison itself, and so will each Christian heart. Believers will be faced with closing the unclean out of their homes and renewing their bonds with God in complete privacy because to do so publicly would invite persecution. Those who do resist the tide will remain civilized men in a tide of barbarism of the sort we see emerging in the young radicals.

There will be a deepening awareness that the personality, the character, of the remaining Christians is fundamentally different from that of secular men. At present, the difference is not very great except in the personalities of the hip kids. The character of the secular liberal is not, at present, noticeably variant from the commited Christian although there is a soft breeze of permissiveness and a relaxation of standards in the liberal, who countenances things the Christian would not, and succumbs to vices that the Christian resists.

That is the revolutionary thing about Christianity: it creates a new, more powerful, more sublime character in the heart of each believer, and this new man has deep political ramifications. The pharisees understood it and demanded the death of Jesus as a radical, a revolutionary. The secular me of our time are beginning to understand it; and when the realization is full upon them, they will begin to persecute the church, even as they now do behind the iron curtain. The Christian character is revolutionary since it recognizes absolute authority beyond the state and beyond consensus. The Christian is governed, in the end, neither by rulers nor public opinion. Moreover, he has self-government within him and needs little state guidance. He is, therefore, suspect to rulers, politicians, and bureaucrats because he has little need for their services. Lacking need for the benevolences of the state, he is ipso facto revolutionary. By contrast the secular man, who has an abiding need for the state to protect him from others and from himself, is the darling of rulers and bureaucrats.

Perhaps the time will soon be at hand when Christianity must retreat into monastic life. Early in the history of the church, St. Benedict organized monastic orders and drew into them those who despaired of life as it existed in the darkening late-Roman world, when all the energies of man seemed to diminish and the lamps of learning and culture seemed one by one to flicker out. The monastics had the common trait of asceticism: they were willing to surrender all worldly gain, and marriage, for a contemplative and spiritual life. For generations they copied and transmitted the sacred texts as well as much of the learning of the ancients, and formed the backbone of the faith when life collapsed into local baronies.

The orders flourished into modern times, but lately have suffered decline in spite of efforts to recruit new brothers and sisters. They can't compete with the attractions of secular life. There are, however, persons of ascetic character who would fit naturally into modern brotherhoods. Some of these have wound up in the Peace Corps or similar secular engines of charity. They are uncomfortable in commerce and prefer a life of service. The orders, on the other hand, have relaxed their rules to encourage outreach and involvement. But the farther they move from the ascetic, contemplative life, the less they seem to attract the spiritual ones who might enter the brotherhoods. True monastics want to be cloistered; their goal is a union with God from morningtide to vespers. There may be a time in the near future, as civilization decays, when the monastic orders are flooded anew with candidates, many of whom will have begun their long spiritual journey in the East Village, or Haight-Asbury.

There is no such refuge as monastic life in the purely scientific and secular world, and that accounts for the deepening terror, and the new versions of apocalypse that are spreading everywhere. Men dream of colonizing a new planet, having despaired of this one. They find no refuge here. At present, there are circulating at least four versions of doom, and the presence of so much doom saying is unique in our times. There is ecological doom: the idea that we will strangle on our own garbage, our filthy water, our poisoned air, and pesticide-laden soil. There is population doom: the idea that we are breeding ourselves into famine, misery, disease, and oblivion. There is nuclear doom: the belief that the squat, ugly rockets in their silos will wipe out civilization and poison the globe with radioactivity. There is the doom of disorder: perverse and corrupt bandits and revolutionaries will shred the whole social structure and reduce man to starvation-haunted serfs terrified of every passing goon. All these versions of terror lie just beyond the campfire in the darkness, paralyzing the huddling mass of men with their wolf-eyes.

At no point in western history have there been so many versions of doom circulating simultaneously as a sort of emotional undertone of the times. One never quite escapes one or another of the versions in everyday life, not even on the happiest of Sunday afternoon picnics. There is the feeling—almost a racial instinct—that we are at the end of an epoch; that these are the last days of life as we know it. People go on living and planning, of course, but the future is opaque, and hope is tempered by the dark visions of calamity squatting across the horizon. For secular men, in particular, these doomsday visions are horrifying: to die a nuclear death; to suffer famine and overcrowding; to choke on the very air, or to find no protection in civilization—all these are monstrous. But while these are

183

equally horrifying to a Christian, he is also a citizen of the City of God, where there will be no famine or terror or death. The Christian, that is, with his dual citizenship, has a haven beyond even death, although such a haven does not make the decay of an epoch less horrifying any more than Noah's ark made the flood less horrifying to Noah.

It is hard to guess whether that buzzing monotone of apocalypse actually affects the behavior of the kids. It used to be popular among students on the make to argue that if the world were going to be blown to smithereens, then let's live and love to the hilt, for who knows whether the sun will rise on the morrow? But that seemed more of a young seducer's argument than any deeply felt cosmic reality. It is true that the young have blotted up the versions of the apocalypse from the media more than their elders, and probably have a deeper despair about the future as a result. Much of what they do seemed grounded in despair. Copping out and radicalism are both responses to despair.

Another version of apocalypse that was prevalent in the fifties and has withered since is the idea of global communism—the triumph of a brutal Red state and the consequent dark ages that would ensue. The idea is no longer in vogue, except on the right, which maintains its wary vigil year after year. But as the years pass, and as the Russian revolution recedes into history, there appears to be a weariness emerging from Russia. The dynamism that so shocked the West is winding down, and while global revolution is pursued still with relentless single-mindedness, there is a sort of ritual quality to it, as though both sides are aware that modern capitalism has rendered the whole Marxist dialectic anachronistic. The communists are today's Victorians, clinging to an elaborate metaphysics in the face of other realities, and ultimately only for the sake of power, rather than the vision of a worker's paradise. Communism will continue to expand into the corrupt free world, but with each expansion it will be drained of its own dynamism and fall prey to its own inertia and suffer its own diminution of energy.

Not even the hip kids and the SDS types are particularly attracted to the great bureaucratic edifice of the Soviet State. The kids prefer the nihilist freedoms of the free world, although there is an undercurrent of hunger for the orderliness of totalitarian society. The god of communism is dead in the young, even if the body lives and flourishes. On the right, the ritual denunciation of atheistic communism has disappeared, and in the churches the sermons no longer dwell upon the menace of Red atheism, but rather on the inner corruption of the American people. We have become introspective, perhaps because even the best Soviet efforts in the realm of diplomacy and propaganda have created little internal menace. The fear may revive when the Soviets achieve strategic military superiority, but until then the Red World is scarcely in the minds of most Americans.

Chairman Mao was wrong. Political power does not stem from the barrel of a gun. It rests in the beliefs of those who hold the guns. Even though New Leftists subscribe in toto to the doctrine of Mao Tse-tung, they do not, in practice, behave according to their doctrine. Their attempts to turn soldiers into peaceniks are, at bottom, efforts to persuade the gun-holders: to subvert their loyalties; to win their allegiance, or, at least, weaken their resolve to obey their commanders. Thus, the New Left is attempting to weaken American military posture not with guns but by persuasion. Chairman Mao was wrong. Political power grows out of belief, or faith if you will, in the rightness of one's ideals. Mao was right only to the extent that sheer terror can hold a nonbeliever in line. The Soviet soldier, for example, may be the victim of the gun-holders. But even in the Soviet Union, the power that governs politics is the fanatical faith of Communist leaders in the rightness of their ideals. The guns are merely tools to enforce that faith.

For that reason the battle for men's minds and hearts always will supersede the struggle to produce the best armies. At present, the only force capable of countering the New Left and converting young radicals to a different life is the church. The state has only guns and propaganda at its disposal and the wild ones have learned how to scotch both. The ultimate confrontation, then, lies not between the radicals and the state but between the radicals and the true Church of Christ. The kids understand that better than the well-insulated squares who have been squandering the sands of time. The whole New Left, ranging from the denizens of Telegraph Avenue south to the Spahn Ranch and the Manson family and through Los Angeles and the East Village, is threaded with devil cults—diabolism, witchcraft, black masses. These are simply the most obvious manifestations of the desire among the kids to be consciously bad; to reject the love of God.

The church is the only puissant opponent of the New Left since it alone retains its values and has the power to resist the diabolism on the left. Conservatives, of course, have a certain political resistance, but they are curiously unable to proselytize the left, or persuade the kids to try another route. It is absurd for such groups as the chambers of commerce or the Daughters of the American Revolution to come armed with a mass of data demonstrating the fecundity and fairness of American capitalism, or the value of working within the system. The kids won't listen to that sort of fascist pig talk. But they did listen to S. I. Hayakawa, acting president of

185

San Francisco State, when he quietly stood up to all their taunts. They would listen to a courageous churchman who would be willing to face death for his troubles. But that churchman could not be a conciliatory type, praising the kids for the evils they do. He would need the courage to rebuke their corruption even while showing them the door to self-acceptance and joy and reverence. He would need the courage of a martyr.

There is coming, perhaps, a time when the church will need martyrs once again. A time when man must be willing to die at the hands of a mob for expounding the joyous doctrine of a loving God and personal redemption. Such a man would not be one to rap with the kids the way some half-apostate clergymen are doing now. There is no rapping with revolutionaries, except by selling out your own faith. Rather, the outreaching church can triumph by teaching faith and love. The kids will demolish all missionaries until one comes who can persuade them that God loves them.

The church is a revolutionary force. It alone profoundly alters the character of individual men and women in society. Ultimately the state and society depend on that good character as a building block in a mild and benevolent order. The church aspires to no political power. Jesus sought something far more significant, the union of man and God which would produce a new type of man on earth. This was His radical program. Power comes not from a gun, but from God. He who is united with God is more powerful than all the armies of the world and their guns; powerful enough to remake the world.

EPILOGUE

THE Kids are calming down. Months ago, when this book was in process, the Kids were implementing their fevered dreams of revolution. There were incessant confrontations between the counterculture and the rest of us. But now the campuses are peaceful. The Kids have burrowed into their books. They are concerned about their careers. To be sure, there were numerous activists for Saint George McGovern, but his minions played it cool through the elections. The New Politics was not significantly different from the old.

All of this, I think, is healthy. However, it does not mean that there is any real change in the ideology governing the youth movement. The Kids still perceive of politics as the salvation of the universe and themselves. They have learned nothing new in the colleges, except the refined art of copulation. Nothing about the faith, hope and joy that springs from the discovery of God. On campuses where the most arcane and esoteric topics are probed religiously, there is no religion. Thus, if anything, the new calm is tactical. It does not represent a strategic shift, although perhaps it is an expression of deepening anomie.

At this writing there is a lamentation in the liberal press about the new "apathy" of the young. The suggestion is made that some dark Nixonian repression is responsible, and that the quietude marks a reversion to the dull, dead Eisenhowerish fifties. If one views the world from the standpoint that politics is good and the feverish militance of the youth is the gateway to paradise, the new calm seems tragic. But I don't share that view. Amidst the calm, I see at every hand the private progress and personal growth that was virtually halted in the militant years. The sudden apathy of the Kids toward the whole gamut of politics marks the beginning of sanity. The Kids remain innately leftist because they never learned alternatives: but politics has been dethroned.

Surely some of the cool can be attributed to the Nixon administration. Unlike its predecessors, it has never aroused pubescent political lusts, nor has it turned its eyes elsewhere when the kids gather to commit mayhem. Neither has the administration held out shimmering promises of utopia: no instant peace; no sudden catapulting of the poor into affluence; no magical solution of racial tensions; no swift abandonment of social traditions. Rather, the Nixon approach has been to perceive and publicize realities: there is a limit beyond which a freeman's government cannot reorder the universe.

The Kids accept that—because they must. But their ideology remains unchanged. They still hate the government, not because it is oppressive, but because it belongs to square America, the America that landslided Mr. Nixon back into office. The Kids still lust for their own turn at the helm.

One reason I doubt that there has been any deep ideological shifting recently is that the counterculture continues to grow. It is co-opting new groups of dissidents, most notably women's lib. It is more than ever grounded on the belief that militance must topple the old order; that tradition is an evil checkrein on the new freedoms. Tradition is what produced male sexist chauvinist pigs; tradition is what created Republicans and poor people. The explosions of the Kid cults in the sixties created a definite, sharp break with the past, and unloosed a torrent of people who will never orient themselves in the traditional society. The great rockfests are over, but the music lingers on.

It is usually possible for a dominant culture or ethic to co-opt its dissidents. But so far, America has not absorbed its counterculture, despite wide-ranging reforms spurred by the young. Despite the fact that campuses have been reformed, taboos and manners changed, and egalitarian programs adopted—despite all that and more, the counterculture remains stubbornly alienated. The Kids may be quiet but they have not been absorbed. I do not believe they can ever be absorbed through traditional reforms. Their rebellion is really not so much against society as against the primal values and sacred beliefs that mold and order society. That is to say, if the Kids have no God, then they cannot be reconciled to a culture that rests—however shakily—on religious foundations. But it is worth remembering that many squares and traditional liberals have no God either, and the day may come when the Jesus People form the principal counterculture tensed against a corrupt mainstream. Some of the kids are not far from God. They scorn the plastic productivity of their grabbing elders and yearn for simpler, purer things. If ever the Kid cults were transformed into a true religious movement, they might become the most beautiful and puissant force of our times. But I doubt that will happen. Too many of the Kids have a compact with the devil.